Anonymous

Murder of Union Soldiers in North Carolina

Letter from the secretary of war, in answer to a resolution of the House of representatives, of April 16

Anonymous

Murder of Union Soldiers in North Carolina
Letter from the secretary of war, in answer to a resolution of the House of representatives, of April 16

ISBN/EAN: 9783337308667

Printed in Europe, USA, Canada, Australia, Japan

Cover: Foto ©ninafisch / pixelio.de

More available books at **www.hansebooks.com**

| 39th Congress, | HOUSE OF REPRESENTATIVES. | Ex. Doc. |
| 1st Session. | | No. 98. |

MURDER OF UNION SOLDIERS IN NORTH CAROLINA.

LETTER

FROM

THE SECRETARY OF WAR,

IN ANSWER TO

A resolution of the House of Representatives, of April 16, transmitting the report of Judge Advocate General Holt, relative to the murder of certain Union soldiers belonging to 1st and 2d North Carolina loyal infantry.

MAY 3, 1866.—Laid on the table and ordered to be printed.

WAR DEPARTMENT,
Washington City, May 2, 1866.

SIR: In reply to the resolution of the House of Representatives, of April 16, 1866, directing the Secretary of War to communicate the Judge Advocate General's report, and other information, respecting measures which have been taken to bring to punishment the murderers of certain Union soldiers belonging to 1st and 2d regiments of North Carolina loyal infantry, alleged to have been tried and executed under orders of the rebel Generals Pickett and Hoke, I have the honor to transmit herewith the Adjutant General's letter of the 1st instant on the subject, covering and enumerating all the papers and correspondence on file in the department.

Very respectfully, sir, your obedient servant,
E. M. STANTON, *Secretary of War.*

Hon. S. COLFAX,
Speaker of the House of Representatives.

ADJUTANT GENERAL'S OFFICE,
Washington, May 1, 1866.

SIR: In compliance with your orders, I have the honor to submit copies of papers called for by resolution of the House of Representatives, dated April 16, 1866, requesting "a report of the Judge Advocate General, and such other information as may be of record or on file in his department, on the subject, which will show what are the facts in the case, and what steps have been taken to bring to justice and punishment the murderers of the following named Union soldiers, belonging to the 1st and 2d regiments of North Carolina loyal infantry, alleged to have been tried and executed by orders of the rebel Generals Pickett and Hoke, under the pretext of their being deserters from the confederate service, viz: Jesse Summerell, Hardy Dougherty, Stephen Jones, David Jones, William Haddock, John Freeman, John Brock, Sergeant Joseph Fulcher, William D. Jones, Charles Cutherall, ——— Kellum, Mitchell Busick, Louis Freeman, Joseph Haskett, Wm. Irvine, Amos Aymett, Stephen H Jones, J. J. Brock."

The papers herewith are:

1. Letter of Major General B. F. Butler to General Grant, enclosing copy of correspondence between Major General J. J. Peck, United States volunteers, and the rebel General Pickett, concerning the execution, &c., of loyal North Carolina Union soldiers.
2. Extracts from North Carolina rebel newspapers.
3. Report of a board of inquiry, and report upon the alleged murder of a large number of United States soldiers by the rebels during the spring of 1864, convened at Newbern, North Carolina, October 19, 1865.
4. Additional proceedings of same court.
5. Proceedings of second board of inquiry in case of murder of Union soldiers at Kinston, North Carolina, in 1864.
6. Report of Judge Advocate General, of December 12, 1865, on memorial and other papers relating to the barbarous slaying upon the gallows of certain Union soldiers at Kinston, North Carolina; papers hereunto appended.
7. Report of Judge Advocate General of December 30, 1865, to the Secretary of War, on the same subject.
8. Letter of Major General J. J. Peck, United States volunteers, of December 22, 1865, to Judge Advocate General.
9. Letter of Judge Advocate General of December 30, 1865, to Secretary of War.
10. Report of a board of inquiry convened at Raleigh, North Carolina, January 17, 1866, in relation to the murder of the United States soldiers by the rebels, in March, April and May, 1864.
11. Abstract of testimony taken before the board of inquiry convened at Raleigh, North Carolina, January 17, 1866, in the matter of the murder of certain United States soldiers, at Kinston, North Carolina, by the rebels in 1864.
12. Letter of Major General Thomas H. Ruger, stating that to enable him to complete the investigation ordered by the Secretary of War, in relation to the murder of certain United States prisoners of war at Kinston, North Carolina, by Pickett and Hoke, he desires to be furnished with copies of certain proceedings of the rebel court-martial which tried said prisoners, with Dr. Francis Lieber's indorsement thereon, stating that these proceedings are not among the records of the archive office.

The papers submitted show that the investigation of this transaction has been continued, under the commanding general department of North Carolina, from the 19th October, 1865, and was progressing until the receipt of the resolution of April 16, with the view of collecting the whole testimony in proper form, for such action as the President might direct.

I am, sir, very respectfully, your obedient servant,

E. D. TOWNSEND,
Assistant Adjutant General.

Hon. E. M. STANTON, *Secretary of War.*

No. 1.

HEADQUARTERS 18TH ARMY CORPS,
DEPARTMENT OF VIRGINIA AND NORTH CAROLINA,
Fortress Monroe, April 14, 1864.

GENERAL: I have the honor to enclose official copies of the correspondence between General Pickett, commanding confederate forces, district of North Carolina, and General Peck, commanding United States forces in said district, relative to the execution of certain prisoners belonging to the second North Carolina regiment.

Many of these men were conscripted by the rebels. All of them were citizens of the United States, who owed their allegiance to our government. If misguided, they forfeited their allegiance, repented, and returned to it again. They have only done their duty, and, in my judgment, are to be protected in so doing.

I do not recognize any right in the rebels to execute a United States soldier, because, either by force or fraud, or by voluntary enlistment even, he has been once brought into their ranks, and has escaped therefrom.

I suppose all the rights they can claim as belligerents is to execute one of the deserters from their army while he holds simply the character of a deserter, during the time he has renounced his allegiance, and before he has again claimed that protection, and it has been accorded to him.

Then, by no law of nations, and by no belligerent rights, have the rebels any power over him, other than to treat him as a prisoner of war, if captured.

I would suggest that the confederate authorities be called upon to say whether they adopt this act, and that upon their answer such action may be taken as will sustain the dignity of the government, and give a promise to afford protection to its citizens.

I have the honor to be, general, very respectfully, your obedient servant,
B. F. BUTLER,
Major General Commanding.

Lieutenant General U. S. GRANT,
Commanding United States Army.

Official copy:
WM. ATWOOD,
Assistant Adjutant General.

HEADQUARTERS ARMY AND DISTRICT OF NORTH CAROLINA,
Newbern, N. C., February 11, 1864.

GENERAL: I have the honor to enclose a slip cut from the Richmond Examiner of February 8, 1864. It is styled "The Advance on Newbern," and appears to have been extracted from the Petersburg Register, a paper published in the city where your headquarters are located.

Your attention is particularly invited to that paragraph which states "that Colonel Shaw was shot dead by a negro soldier from the other side of the river, which he was spanning with a pontoon bridge, and that the negro was watched and followed, taken and hanged, after the action of Thomasville."

"THE ADVANCE ON NEWBERN."

"The Petersburg Register gives the following additional particulars of the advance on Newbern: Our army, according to the report of passengers arriving from Weldon, has fallen back to a point sixteen miles west of Newbern.

"The reason assigned for this retrograde movement was, that Newbern could not be taken by us without a loss on our part which would find no equivalent in its capture, as the place was stronger than we anticipated. Yet, in spite of all this, we are sure the expedition will result in good to our cause. Our forces are now in a situation to get large supplies from a country still abundant, to prevent raids on points westward, and keep tories in check, and hang them when caught.

"From a private, who was one of the guard that brought the batch of prisoners through, we learn that Colonel Shaw was shot dead by a negro soldier from the other side of the river, which he was spanning with a pontoon bridge. The negro was watched, followed, taken, and hanged after the action at Thomasville. It is stated that when our troops entered Thomasville a number of the enemy took shelter in the houses and fired upon them. The Yankees were ordered to surrender, but refused, whereupon our men set fire to the houses, and their occupants got bodily a taste, in this world, of the 'flames eternal.'"

The government of the United States has wisely seen fit to enlist many thousand colored soldiers to aid in putting down the revolution, and has placed them on the same footing, in all respects, as her white troops. The orders of the President on this subject are so just, full, and clear, that I enclose a copy for your information:

[General Orders No. 252.]

WAR DEPARTMENT, ADJUTANT GENERAL'S OFFICE,
Washington, July 31, 1863.

The following order from the President is published for the information and government of all concerned:

"EXECUTIVE MANSION,
"*Washington, D. C., July* 20, 1863.

"It is the duty of every government to give protection to its citizens, of whatever class, color or condition, and especially to those organized as soldiers in the public service. The law of nations and the usages and customs of war, as carried on by civilized powers, permit no distinction as to color in the treatment of prisoners of war as public enemies. To sell or enslave any captured person on account of his color, and for no offence against the laws of war, is a relapse in barbarism, and a crime against the civilization of the age.

"The government of the United States will give the same protection to all its soldiers; and if the enemy shall sell or enslave any one because of his color, the offence shall be punished by retaliation upon the enemy's prisoners in our possession.

"It is therefore ordered, that for every soldier of the United States killed in violation of the laws of war, a rebel soldier shall be executed; and for every one enslaved by the enemy or sold into slavery, a rebel soldier shall be placed at hard labor on the public works, and continued on such labor, until the other shall be released, and receive the treatment due to a prisoner of war.

"ABRAHAM LINCOLN.
"By order of the Secretary of War:
"E. D. TOWNSEND,
"*Assistant Adjutant General.*"

Believing that this atrocity has been perpetrated without your knowledge, and that you will take prompt steps to disavow this violation of the usages of war, and to bring the offenders to justice, I shall refrain from executing a rebel soldier until I learn your action in the premises.

I am, very respectfully, your obedient servant,
JOHN J. PECK, *Major General.*
Major General PICKETT,
Dep't of Va. and N. C., Confederate Army, Petersburg.

HEADQUARTERS ARMY AND DISTRICT OF NORTH CAROLINA,
Newbern, N. C., February 13, 1864.

GENERAL: I have the honor to enclose a list of fifty-three soldiers of the United States government who are supposed to have fallen into your hands in your late hasty retreat from before Newbern.

They are loyal and true North Corolinians, and duly enlisted in the 2d North Carolina infantry. I ask for them the same treatment, in all respects, as you will mete out to other prisoners of war.

I am, very respectfully, your obedient servant,

JOHN J. PECK, *Major General.*

Major General PICKETT,
Department of Virginia and North Carolina, Confederate Army.

HEADQUARTERS DEPARTMENT OF NORTH CAROLINA,
Petersburg, Va., February 16, 1864.

GENERAL: Your communication of the 11th of February is received. I have the honor to state, in reply, that the paragraph from a newspaper enclosed therein is not only without foundation in fact, but so ridiculous that I should scarcely have supposed it worthy of consideration; but I would respectfully inform you that had I caught any negro who had killed officer, soldier, or citizen of the Confederate States, I should have caused him to be immediately executed.

To your threat expressed in the following extract from your communication, viz: "Believing that this atrocity has been perpetrated without your knowledge, and that you will take prompt steps to disavow this violation of the usages of war, and to bring the offenders to justice, I shall refrain from executing a rebel soldier until I learn your action in the premises," I have merely to say that I have in my hands and subject to my orders, captured in the recent operations in this department, some 450 officers and men of the United States army, and for every man you hang, I will hang ten of the United States army.

I am, general, very respectfully, your obedient servant,

G. E. PICKETT,
Major General, Commanding.

Major General JOHN J. PECK,
United States Army, Commanding at Newbern.

HEADQUARTERS DEPARTMENT OF NORTH CAROLINA,
Petersburg, Va., February 17, 1864.

GENERAL: Your communication of the 13th instant is at hand. I have the honor to state, in reply, that you have made a slight mistake in regard to numbers; three hundred and twenty-five having "fallen into (our) your hands in (our) your late hasty retreat from before Newbern," instead of the list of fifty-three with which you so kindly furnished me, and which will enable me to bring to justice many who have up to this time escaped their just deserts.

I herewith return you the names of those who have been tried and convicted by court-martial for desertion from the confederate service; and taken with arms in hand, "duly enlisted in the 2d North Carolina infantry, United States army," they have been duly executed according to law and the custom of war.

Your letter and list will, of course, prevent any mercy being shown any of the remaining number, should proper and just proof be brought of their having deserted the confederate colors.

Many of these men plead in extenuation that they have been forced into the ranks of the federal government.

Extending to you my thanks for your opportune list,

I remain, very respectfully, your obedient servant,

G. E. PICKETT.
Major General, Commanding.

Major General JOHN J. PECK,
Commanding U. S. Forces, Newbern, N. C.

List of prisoners captured before Newbern and executed at Kinston, North Carolina, as deserters from the confederate army:

David Jones, J. L. Haskett, John L. Stanley, Lewis Bryan, Mitchell Busick, William Irving, Amos Armyett, John J. Beck, William Haddick, Jesse Summerlin, Andrew J. Brittian, William Jones, Lewis Freeman, Calvin Hoffman, Stephen Jones, Joseph Biock, Lewis Taylor, Charles Cuthrell, William H. Doughtry, John Freeman, Elijah Kellum, William J. Hill.

HEADQUARTERS ARMY AND DISTRICT OF NORTH CAROLINA,
Newbern, N. C., February 20, 1864.

GENERAL: Soon after your retreat from Newbern, I had the honor to address you respecting fifty-three loyal North Carolinians who had fallen into your hands. They having been duly enlisted into the 2d North Carolina regiment, I asked for them the treatment of prisoners of war.

Your attention is called to the enclosed slip cut from the Fayetteville Observer of February 8, 1864, setting forth that some of the prisoners taken near Newbern have been executed, which I hope will prove to be unfounded.

"*Traitors executed.*—Among the prisoners captured by our forces near Newbern were several deserters from our army. We learn by an officer just from the spot that two of these have already been executed, and others are undergoing trial."

Having reported this matter to higher authority, I am instructed to notify you, that if the members of the North Carolina regiment who have been captured are not treated as prisoners of war, the strictest retaliation will be enforced.

Two colonels, two lieutenant colonels, two majors, and two captains are held at Fort Monroe as hostages for their safety.

These officers have not been placed in close custody, because the authorities do not believe that any harm is intended by you to the members of 2d North Carolina regiment.

I am, very respectfully, your obedient servant,
JOHN J. PECK, *Major General.*
Major General PICKETT,
Confederate Army, Petersburg.

HEADQUARTERS ARMY AND DISTRICT OF NORTH CAROLINA,
Newbern, N. C., February 27, 1864.

GENERAL: February 13th I had the honor to address you in respect to fifty-three North Carolinians who had fallen into your hands in your late operations about Newbern. As they were truly loyal men, who had duly enlisted in the United States army, I requested the same treatment of them as should be meted out to other prisoners of war. No allusion was made to the question of your right to place these men upon any other footing, or to the matter of retaliation.

In your reply of the 17th you enclosed a list of twenty-two who have been executed at Kinston, and express the determination to punish the balance if proof is found of their desertion from your service.

These men, in common with more than half of the population of the State, were ever loyal to the United States, and opposed secession until put down by arbitrary power. A merciless conscription drove them into the service, and for a time compelled the suspense of their real sentiments, but was powerless to destroy their love for the federal Union. With tens of thousands they seized the first opportunity to rush within my lines, and resume their former allegiance. Had these men been traitors to the United States at the outburst of the rebellion, their claims upon it for protection and sympathy, under the circumstances, would not have been strong; but, in view of their unswerving and unflagging loyalty, I cannot doubt that the government will take immediate steps to redress these outrages upon humanity, and to correct such gross violations of usages of civilized warfare. In any event, my duty has been performed, and the blood of these unfortunates will rest upon you and your associates.

In your communication of the 16th you threaten to execute ten of the officers and soldiers of the United States army for every one of your men, prisoners in my hands, which I shall execute under the orders of the President of the United States, which I enclose for your information. This announcement, taken in connexion with the execution of the North Carolinians, and similar proceedings elsewhere, evinces a most extraordinary thirst for life and blood on the part of the confederate authorities. Such violent and revengeful acts resorted to as a show of strength are the best evidences of the weak and crumbling condition of the confederacy.

This wicked rebellion has now attained that desperate state which history shows is always the shortest of revolutionary stages. The friends of the Union, everywhere, truly interpret these signs of madness and recklessness, and are now making one grand rally for the utter overthrow and final extinction of all treason.

Very respectfully, your obedient servant,
JOHN J. PECK, *Major General.*

Major General GEO. E. PICKETT,
Department of North Carolina, Confederate Army.

Official copy:

W. M. ATWOOD,
Assistant Adjutant General.

HEADQUARTERS ARMY AND DISTRICT NORTH CAROLINA,
Newbern, N. C., February 9, 1864.

GENERAL: A few days since, while the forces under your command were in front of this place, I sent a medical officer with some ambulances to the small-pox hospital, near which some of your forces had arrived, with a flag, for the sole purpose of bringing away the unfortunate occupants of the building, as, in case of an attack on my lines, they would certainly be in great danger of having their house burned over their heads. Besides, I had no desire to see the loathsome disease spread among your own forces, and it was proper that you should be put on your guard as to the nature of the hospital. The medical officer who went on this humane errand was instructed, of course, to explain these matters to any of your forces that he might meet, and he doubtless did so. He was, however, seized and carried away as a prisoner, with the ambulances and drivers.

I have known you too long and too well to believe that this could have been done by your directions, or by your knowledge, and I respectfully request you to do what I feel certain I would do myself under the circumstances—that is, return the surgeon and the drivers to me. The ambulances and horses I say nothing of, for they are too trifling to me to mention. Hoping that you will see the impropriety of punishing this little party for a humane act, and that you will be willing to meet me half way in these little amenities of war,

I remain, very respectfully, your obedient servant,
J. V. PALMER,
Brigadier General U. S. A., Commanding.

Major General GEO. E. PICKETT,
C. S. A., Commanding in North Carolina.

The surgeon is Assistant Surgeon R. S. Baker, 12th New York cavalry. The drivers are Private Calvin D. Willis, company K, 17th Massachusetts volunteers; Private Henry Taylor, company G, 17th Massachusetts volunteers; Private Edward Murry, company C, 158th New York volunteers; Private Edward Moore, company E, 19th Wisconsin volunteers.

HEADQUARTERS DEPARTMENT OF NORTH CAROLINA,
February 17, 1864.

GENERAL: I have the honor to acknowledge your very courteous communication of the 9th instant, in relation to Surgeon Baker, 12th New York cavalry. The case was duly and immediately reported to me by Major Read, C. S. A., who took charge of the medical officer and party.

They came with no flag of truce, and therefore could not be recognized; in addition, the surgeon, by his inquiries, conversation, and observation, had learned too much to render his return desirable. I fully appreciate, general, your kind remarks and remembrances in relation to myself, but you are probably not aware that on many fields of battle medical officers of my division have, when left in charge of wounded, been seized upon and kept as prisoners under close guard. No one reprobates such a method of warfare more than I do, but we did not initiate it. I shall take pleasure in forwarding your polite communication to the proper authorities at Richmond, suggesting, upon your statement, the release of the parties named.

I am, general, very respectfully, your obedient servant,
G. E. PICKETT,
Major General, Commanding.

Brigadier General J. V. PALMER, U. S. A.

Official:

W. A. NICHOLS,
Assistant Adjutant General.

HEADQUARTERS DEPARTMENT OF NORTH CAROLINA,
Temporarily at Goldsborough, February 17, 1864.

GENERAL: I have the honor to transmit copies of letters received from Generals Peck and Palmer at Newbern also my replies to the same.

The packages intended for the prisoners are forwarded, all having been first examined. Two of the notes are evidently counterfeit; the letter from Lieutenant Kirby's father is worth perusing.

The surgeon and his party referred to were taken up without a flag, and had obtained too much information to be trusted to return under any circumstances at that time. It remains with the department to examine into the just merits in the matter of exchanging or returning them. I suggest the latter.

I am, general, very respectfully, you obedient servant,
G. E. PICKETT,
Major General, Commanding.

General S. COOPER,
Adjutant and Inspector General, Richmond, Va.

Official:

W. A. NICHOLS,
Assistant Adjutant General.

MURDER OF UNION SOLDIERS IN NORTH CAROLINA.

HEADQUARTERS DEPARTMENT OF NORTH CAROLINA,
Petersburg, Va., February 26, 1864.

GENERAL: I have the honor to enclose copies of letters from Generals Peck and Palmer, and my answers; likewise my letter to you of the 17th instant, forwarding the same. I am sorry to say the courier, Private J. L. Watkins, 18th Virginia, deserted to the enemy. He did not, however, take any valuable information. I send by Captain Bright, my aide-de-camp, the money to Lieutenant Kirby, as it will not do for this officer to lose what was entrusted to my charge, I feeling myself in honor bound. The clothing I have recovered a portion of, and send on.

I also enclose, general, copy of letter to-day received from General Peck. I have not answered it yet; think the most direct way will be by next flag-of-truce boat. You will perceive that these men were hung by sentence of general court-martial regularly appointed. If these colonels, lieutenant colonels, and captains, of whom he speaks, are deserters from the federal army, he can execute them; otherwise, it will be murder. I hope the whole of the prisoners captured in this department will be held at my disposal.

The officers General Peck speaks of were not taken here. My letter of the 15th, enclosing correspondence between myself and General Peck, has not been answered. I respectfully ask a reply from the Secretary.

I am, general, very respectfully, your obedient servant,
G. E. PICKETT,
Major General, Commanding.

General S. COOPER,
Adjutant and Inspector General.

Official:
W. A. NICHOLS,
Assistant Adjutant General.

HEADQUARTERS DEPARTMENT OF NORTH CAROLINA,
Petersburg, Va., February 27, 1864.

GENERAL: Your communication of the 20th instant is received. Your letter of the 13th, referred to, was received and replied to, by flag, under date of 17th.

You have doubtless perused my reply ere this, and are aware of the fact that the men "duly enlisted into the 2d North Carolina regiment," spoken of by you, had been duly enlisted in the confederate service previously, and had deserted from same; that they were taken in arms fighting against their colors, were tried by a duly organized court, sentenced and executed.

If the officers of the Confederate States army, whom you speak of as hostages for their safety, can be proven to be deserters from the federal army, you will certainly be fully justified in treating them similarly; otherwise, should you retaliate, you will simply be guilty of murder.

The subject does not, however, admit of discussion, and I refer you to the concluding paragraph of my letter of the 16th instant.

I am, general, very respectfully, your obedient servant,
G. E. PICKETT, *Major General.*

Major General JOHN PECK,
United States Army.

Official:
W. A. NICHOLS,
Assistant Adjutant General.

HEADQUARTERS DEPARTMENT OF NORTH CAROLINA,
March 15, 1864.

GENERAL: The communication you have done me the honor to address, under date of February 27, is at hand. Having nothing in it which, as I conceive, has any noticeable bearing upon the matters first advanced by you, and being in fact merely an opinion of your own, intended entirely to gain favor with your superiors at your seat of government, I merely deem it necessary to acknowledge its receipt.

I am, general, very respectfully, your obedient servant,
G. E. PICKETT,
Major General, Commanding.

Major General J. J. PECK,
  Commanding United States Forces, Newbern, N. C.

Official:

C. PICKETT,
Assistant Adjutant General.

A true copy:

G. NORMAN LIEBER,
Brevet Lieutenant Colonel.

Official:

W. A. NICHOLS,
Assistant Adjutant General.

HEADQUARTERS DEPARTMENT OF NORTH CAROLINA,
Petersburg, Va., March 25, 1864.

GENERAL: I have the honor to enclose copy of letter from General J. J. Peck, and my answer to same; and am, general,
  Very respectfully, your obedient servant,
G. E. PICKETT,
Major General, Commanding.

General S. COOPER,
  A. and I. G., C S. A., Richmond, Va.

A true copy:

G. NORMAN LIEBER,
Brevet Lieutenant Colonel.

Official:

W. A. NICHOLS,
Assistant Adjutant General.

No. 2.

[Extract from "The Weekly Register," Petersburg, Va., Friday morning, November 6, 1863.]

MILITARY DEPARTMENT OF NORTH CAROLINA, Major General G. E. PICKETT, commanding.

Staff officers.—Major Charles Pickett, A. A. S., chief of staff; Major Walter Harrison, assistant adjutant and inspector general; Captain E. R. Baird, A. D. C.; Captain W. Stuart Symington, A. D. C.; Captain R. A. Bright, A. D. C.; Captain S. G. Leitch, chief of ordnance; Major R. F. Scott, chief quartermaster;

Major H. W. Jones, chief commissary of subsistence; Surgeon M. M. Lewis, chief surgeon; Captain Raymond Fairfax, chief of pioneer party; Lieutenant John R. Gossett, provost marshal; Lieutenant J. S. Morson, engineer; Major —— Keer, commandant post; Major E. B. Branch, post quartermaster; Captain J. B. Read, post commissary of subsistence; Surgeon —— —— Douglas, post surgeon; Major Geo. C. Cobell, 18th Virginia regiment, provost marshal of city.

Official:

W. A. NICHOLS,
Assistant Adjutant General.

[Extract from the "Fayetteville Observer," Fayetteville, North Carolina, February 8, 1864.]

TRAITORS EXECUTED.

Among the prisoners captured by our forces near Newbern were several deserters from our army. We learn by an officer just from the spot that two of these have already been executed, and others are undergoing trial.

Official:

W. A. NICHOLS,
Assistant Adjutant General.

[Extracts from the "Weekly Confederate," Raleigh, Wednesday, February 17, 1864.]

PUBLIC EXECUTION.

J. S. Stanley, Lewis Bryan, Mitchell Busick, William Irvin, and Amos Amyett, of Nethercutt's battalion, lately found as deserters to the enemy, have been tried and hanged, thus paying with their lives the penalty of their shocking crime. These men, we believe, were from the county of Jones. They were poor and ignorant men; but some of them had near relatives, and all of them had friends. The hearts of their kindred have been sore stricken by their sad and disgraceful end. Are they only to blame? They left the service, and assumed that of the enemy, on the plea of some fancied wrong done by our government in the removal of Colonel Nethercutt's command from the outpost service, in which they were engaged in Jones and Onslow counties, into General Martin's, and the ordering them to Wilmington. This slight supposed grievance furnished the excuse for their great crime; but was there no newspaper which, circulating in that section, aggravated to their eyes the injury they complained of? Did no newspaper take *also* the ground that the government had committed towards them a breach of faith? If there were, then *that paper* exceeded the liberty of the press, to interfere, wantonly and injuriously, with the military movements. That paper instigated the crime, and is responsible for the consequences its teaching has produced. When any person gives counsel which leads immediately to the commission of felony, that person is an accessory before the fact.

If these poor, deluded men have friends or kin—and we know Colonel Nethercutt at least to be their friend so far as to see that they have justice—they ought to search the press; and if it be found that pernicious counsels have led to this deplorable crime and its attending calamity, the blood of these men appeals for justice upon all guilty—the instigator as well as the actor.

[Army correspondence of the Richmond Sentinel.]

THE OPERATIONS BEFORE NEWBERN.

KINSTON, N. C., *February* 8, 1864.

* * * * * * * * *

Among the captives were some who had deserted our army and joined the enemy. They were easily identified, and two of them have been court-martialled and hung, while some ten or twelve others are awaiting sentence to expiate their crimes, and end their infamy upon the gallows.

Official:

W. A. NICHOLS,
Assistant Adjutant General.

[Extract from the "Western Democrat," Charlotte, North Carolina, Tuesday, February 23, 1864.]

TRAITORS EXECUTED.

J. S. Stanley, L. Bryan, Mitchell Busic, William Irvin, and Ymos Armyett, of Nethercutt's battalion, who had deserted their colors and gone to the Yankees and taken up arms against their land and kindred, were hanged in Kinston on the 21st instant. The prisoners were accompanied to the gallows by Hoke's and Bartow's brigades. They ascended the scaffold with a firm and elastic step, and seemed to bear up under their trials with much fortitude. They had but little to say, except Busick, who entreated his old comrades in arms to stand by their flag and never desert it under any circumstances whatever, lest they should come to the ignominous end of those who were then about to die the felon's death and fill a felon's grave. "Oh, that I had never been born," one of the prisoners was heard to exclaim in his anguish a moment before the trap fell.

(Correspondence of the Raleigh Confederate.)

Official:

W. A. NICHOLS.
Assistant Adjutant General.

[Extract from the "Wilmington Journal," Confederate States of America, Wilmington, North Carolina, Tuesday morning, April 28, 1864.]

THE DESERTERS HUNG AT KINSTON, NORTH CAROLINA.

We find in the North Carolina Presbyterian a long letter from the Rev. John Parris, chaplain of the 54th regiment North Carolina troops, giving a detailed account of the capture, conviction, and hanging of twenty-two deserters at Kinston. We make the following extracts:

"In our late campaign against Newbern we captured in the ranks of the enemy, with arms in their hands, and dressed out in the Yankee toggery, twenty-two men who were recognized and proved to be deserters from the confederate service. They have all been tried by court-martial, found guilty, condemned and suffered the penalty of death upon the gallows. They were all turned over to our brigade for execution. At the instance of Brigadier General Hoke, I attended them in confinement, in the character of a minister of the Gospel, and accompanied them to the gallows. Thus I learned their history and heard their confessions. On Friday, the 5th instant, Joseph L. Hasket and David Jones, of Craven county, who deserted from the 10th regiment, were executed.

"They were illiterate men; neither of them could read. Admitted they had deserted, but insisted that the Yankees compelled them to take the oath and enlist. These were the most unfeeling and hardened men I have ever encountered. They had been raised up in ignorance and vice. They manifested but little, if any, concern about eternity. They marched to the gallows with apparent indifference. Jones, though quite a young man, never shed a tear. By deserting the flag of their country they were guilty of perjury, but they seemed to regard it with indifference. With this state of feeling they were launched into eternity.

"On Friday, the 12th, five more of the prisoners were brought to the scaffold. As all of these executions had to take place within twenty-four hours after the publication of their sentence, I had only that space of time to devote to their religious instruction before they went to the bar of God. The names of these men were Amos Armyett, William Irving, Mitchell Busick, Lewis Bryan, and John Stanley, all deserters from Nethercutt's battalion and from Jones county. Upon entering the cell in which they were confined, I asked if any of them were members of the church? Armyett replied that he was, and had been a Methodist for years; that he was prepared to meet his judge in peace. But as I don't admit a man's lips as test of his Christianity, I thought them only as sinners against God of the most heaven-defying character. I urged upon them the importance of making a full and complete confession of all their sins before both God and man ; yet I am afraid these men were willing to look the great sin of perjury, of which they were guilty, fully in the face. Yet each one, before starting to the gallows, professed to have made his peace with his God, and two of them were baptized in the Christian faith. I suggested to them that they owed to their fellow men one duty, viz: that they should give to me the names of the men who had seduced them to desert and go to the enemy. This they readily assented to, and gave me the names of five citizens of Jones county as the authors of their ruin, disgrace, and death, which names I took down in writing, and handed it into the general's office, and they will no doubt be properly attended to. At the gallows Armyett, who was the eldest of the five, made, as chief speaker, the following confession, written down as delivered :

"'I believe my peace is made with God. I did wrong in volunteering after I got to Newbern. I would rather have laid in jail all my life than have done it. I have rendered prayer unto God to forgive my sin. I trust in him, and in him only.' (The prisoners said, we all feel the same way.)

"Mitchell Busick said: 'I went to Newbern and they (the Yankees) told me if I did not go into their service I should be taken through the lines and shot. In this way I was frightened into it.' They all declared: 'We wish a statement made to the North Carolina troops that we have done wrong and regret it; and warn others not to follow our example.'

*　　*　　*　　*　　*　　*　　*　　*

"On Monday, the 15th instant, thirteen more marched to the gallows. I made my first visit to them, as chaplain, on Sunday morning. The scene beggars all description. Some of them were comparatively young men ; but they had made the fatal mistake ; they had only twenty-four hours to live, and but little preparation had been made for death. Here was a wife to say farewell to a husband forever. Here a mother to take the last look at her ruined son ; and then a sister who had come to embrace, for the last time, the brother who had brought disgrace upon the very name she bore, by his treason to his country. I told them they had sinned against their country, and that country would not forgive; but they had also sinned against God, yet God would forgive if they approached him with penitent hearts filled with a godly sorrow for sin, and repose their trust in the atoning blood of Christ. They gave, apparently, marked attention to my ministration of the word and of prayer. On the next morning, before they were carried to the scaffold, I visited them again and had with me as companions Rev. Mr. Thompson, chaplain of the 43d, Rev. Mr. Schenk, of Guilford county, Rev. Mr. Hines, missionary to brigade, and Rev. R. R. Michaux, North Carolina conference. After reading a chapter and prayer, I administered the ordinance of Christian baptism to eight of these poor condemned wretches, after the manner that Paul and Silas administered it to the jailer and his household, in the prison at midnight, in Philippi. They had received no religious visit from any one except the one from myself the preceding morning, and one in the afternoon, at my request, from Rev. Mr. Thompson. I administered baptism at the request made on the morning before.

* * * * * * *

"The thirteen marched to the gallows with apparent resignation. Some of them I hope were prepared for their doom. Others I fear not. On the scaffold they were all arranged in one row. At a given signal the trap fell, and they were in eternity in a few moments. The scene was truly appalling; but it was as truly the deserters' doom. Many of them said I never expected to come to such an end as this. But yet they were deserters, and as such they ought to have expected such a doom. The names of these misguided men were John J. Brock, Wm. Haddock, Jesse Summerlin, A. J. Brittain, Wm. Jones, Lewis Freeman, Calvin Huffman, Stephen Jones, Joseph Brock, Lewis Taylor, Charles Cuthrell, W. C. Daughtry and John Freeman. Ten of them were deserters from Nethercutt's battalion.

"On yesterday, the 22d, William J. Hill and Elijah Kellum were carried to the gallows, and hanged as deserters. Kellum was quite a young man, unable to read, but guilty of the dreadful crime according to his own showing. He professed to die in peace, and received the ordinance of baptism before death. The other looked very much like an impenitent man, and died leaving a wife and three helpless children to bear the disgrace of his heavy crime unto the third and the fourth generation."

Official:

W. A. NICHOLS,
Assistant Adjutant General.

No. 3.

Report of a board of inquiry, and report upon the alleged murder of a large number of United States soldiers by the rebels during the spring of 1864, convened by the following order:

[Special Order No. 217.—Extract.]

HEADQUARTERS DEPARTMENT OF NORTH CAROLINA,
Raleigh, N. C., October 19, 1865.

A board, to consist of the following named officers, is hereby appointed to meet at Newbern, North Carolina, on Monday, October 23, 1865, or as soon thereafter as practicable, to inquire into and report upon the circumstances connected with the alleged murder of a large number of United States soldiers by the rebels during the months of March, April, and May, 1864; the junior member will act as recorder: Captain W. H. Doherty, assistant quartermaster; Captain Burton S. Mills, 14th United States colored artillery, heavy; 2d Lieutenant Jonathan Hopkins, 14th United States colored artillery, heavy.

By command of Brevet Major General Ruger:

J. A. CAMPBELL,
Assistant Adjutant General

GENERAL: The board met pursuant to the above order on Monday, October 23, 1865, when, after being duly constituted agreeably to paragraphs 1 and 3, Revised Army Regulations, 93d article of war, proceeded to business.

The president of the board read a memorial relative to the murder of United States soldiers at Kinston, North Carolina, upon which the action of the board was to be based. There being no witnesses before the board, it proceeded to summons such persons as were set forth in the memorial as being cognizant to the facts under consideration; after which the board adjourned until October 31, 1865, to await the appearance of witnesses.

The board met pursuant to adjournment. Present, the president and all the members. The board then proceeded to the examination of witnesses. After examining a large number (28) of witnesses, who were most familiar with the facts connected with the alleged murder, and also such persons as were within reach of the board who were most likely to be acquainted with the persons and circumstances conniving at the death of these United States soldiers, the board have the honor to make the following report, comprising facts and inferences deduced from the testimony, viz: There was a large number of United States soldiers hung at Kinston, North Carolina, by the rebels during the months of February and March, 1864. There is a discrepancy in the testimony as to the number of men executed, but the testimony is substantially as follows:

The rebels executed twenty-three or four men, said to have been United States soldiers, at Kinston, North Carolina; (testimony of ———— ————.) About twenty United States soldiers were executed by the rebels at Kinston, North Carolina, as follows: Two men were hung first, thirteen next, and five lastly according to the best of memory; (testimony of Josiah Wood.) Other evidence shows twenty-two United States soldiers to have been hung. Two were at first executed together, afterwards thirteen, and lastly seven; (testimony of W. F. Huggins.) All the testimony agrees that there were three separate executions, and also that the number hung at the first two executions were two and thirteen; and in the opinion of the board seven is the number of those who were victims of the last execution which gives a total of twenty-two.

The first of these executions, was performed some time between the 1st and 15th of February, 1864; the second on the 15th February, 1864; and the last some time in the month of March, 1864. (Testimony of D. S. Brock.)

The victims of this outrage were taken prisoners by the rebels from the 2d North Carolina Union volunteers, at Beech Grove, North Carolina, on or about the 1st of February, 1864, while engaged, under command of United States officers, in opposing the rebels under command of the rebel General Pickett.

The following are the names of persons proven to have been murdered as above stated, viz: 1, Wm. D. Haddock; 2, Wm. Jones; 3, W. H. Dougherty; 4, John J. Brock; 5, Jesse J. Summerlin; 6, Stephen Jones; 7, Joseph Brock; 8, Andrew J. Britton; (testimony of A. N. Daniels;) 9, John Freeman; 10, Mitchell Busick; 11, Wm. L. Bryan; 12, Wm. Irvine; 13, Elijah Kellum; 14, John Stanley; 15, Lewis Freeman; 16, Amos Amyett; (testimony of Isaiah Wood;) 17, William J. Hill; (testimony of Wm. J. Pope;) 18, Lewis Taylor; 19, David Jones; (testimony of Daniel S. Brock;) 20, Calvin J. Houghman; 21, Charles Catherell; (testimony of Wm. Fields.)

The following list of names includes all the enlisted men of the 2d North Carolina Union volunteers known and believed to have been hung by the rebels, viz: 1, Wm. D. Haddock; 2, Wm. Jones; 3, Wm. H. Dougherty; 4, John J. Brock; 5, John Freeman; 6, Mitchell Busick; 7, Wm. L. Bryan; 8, Wm. Irvine; 9, Wm. J. Hill; 10, Lewis Taylor; 11, Calvin J. Houghman; 12, Jesse J. Summerlin; 13, Joseph Brock; 14, Andrew J. Britton; 15, Stephen Jones; 16, Elijah Kellum; 17, John Stanley; 18, Lewis Freeman; 19, Amos Amyett; 20, David Jones; 21, Charles Catherell; 22, Joseph Hasket.

The evidence shows the following named persons to have been members of the 2d North Carolina Union volunteers: 1, Joseph L. Hasket; 2, Mitchell Busick; 3, Willian Irvine; 4, Amos Amyett; 5, David Jones; 6, Lewis Bryan; 7, John J. Brock; 8, Wm. D. Haddock; 9, Jesse J. Summerlin; 10, Andrew J. Britton; 11, Lewis Freeman; 12, Calvin J. Houghman; 13, Stephen Jones; 14, Joseph Brock; 15, Lewis Taylor; 16, Charles Cutherell; 17, Wm. H. Dougherty; 18, Elijah Kellum; (testimony of Lieutenant W. H. Eddins, formerly acting sergeant major of 2d North Carolina volunteers;) 19, John Stanley; 20, John Freeman; (testimony of C. C. Phillips.)

These several lists show these facts: first, that the testimony fixes the fact definitely that twenty-one men were executed, by designating them by name, and that the man not so proven is known as Joseph Hasket; second, that twenty of these men have been members of the 2d North Carolina Union volunteers, and that the names of those said to have been executed who have not been proved to have been United States soldiers are Joseph Hasket and Wm. Jones.

After the capture of these men at Beech Grove, North Carolina, they were confined in the court-house at Kinston, North Carolina, until they were removed to the dungeon of the old jail at the same town, (testimony of Mrs. Elizabeth Jones,) where they remained until they were executed under most cruel and debasing treatment, and were rescued from starvation only by their friends supplying them with food. (Testimony of Celia J. Brock.) Nor did the outrages perpetrated upon the victims of the wholesale slaughter cease with cruel treatment or with death itself; these dead bodies were stripped of their clothing almost or quite to a state of nudity. (testimony of Mrs. Nancy Jones and others,) to be contemptously left for relatives to gather up and inter, delivered to experimenting surgery, like a common felon, or scooped into a common grave at the foot of the gallows, while their families were insulted, robbed of their property, and left to depend upon the charity of friends, (while they who befriended them were themselves in danger,) or suffer for a mere subsistence. (Testimony of Catherine Summerlin.)

These men were tried by a rebel court-martial convened at Kinston, North Carolina, for that purpose, (testimony of J. A. Parrott, G. W. Cox, and others,) but the board has been unable to learn who comprised this court, or by whose order it was convened, though it was thought to have been comprised of officers (rebels) belonging to Virginia organizations, and the fact that officers from North Carolina, stationed at Kinston, North Carolina, at the time, were not able to testify concerning them, leads to the inference that they were appointed by General Pickett, (department commander,) from his division of Virginia rebel troops, enlisted for confederate service. These men were arraigned and tried upon the charge of *desertion*. (Testimony of A. N. Daniels.)

The testimony of J. H. Nethercutt proves, conclusively, that these men belonged to the local North Carolina service, and that they never had been confederate soldiers; therefore, in the opinion of the board, a Confederate States court-martial had no jurisdiction over them; and, further, the court-martial virtually acknowledged its incapacity in the case of Clinton Cox, who was arraigned upon the same charge, but who, it appears, was saved from the fate of the others by the testimony of a Captain G. W. Cox, (captain of a local North Carolina company,) which was to the effect that Clinton Cox had belonged to his company, but that he had not deserted, because he did not consider leaving a local company desertion from confederate service. (Testimony of G. W. Cox.) Witnesses and counsel were denied to other men, and they were hung, (testimony of Bryan McCullen,) while their cases were parallel but less aggravated. It is the opinion of the board that further investigation would prove that Elijah Kellum never had been either in the local or confederate service, but that he was fraudulently reported as conscripted by a Captain Wilson, of Jones county, North Carolina, enrolling officer in the rebel service.

The rebel General Pickett was in command of the department of eastern North Carolina, (testimony of O. S. Dewey,) and approved the sentence of death passed by the above-mentioned court, and ordered the execution of these United States soldiers, (testimony of W. J. Tops, Geo. W. Camp,) and General Hoke, in command of Kinston, North Carolina, was charged with the execution, (testimony of J. H. Nethercutt,) by the agency of Pickett's provost guard and several voluntary hangmen, one of whom is known as Blunt King, of Goldsborough, North Carolina. (Testimony of Isaiah Wood, D. S. Brock, and others.) The person who hung the thirteen is known as a tall, dark-complexioned man, with a cross or squint eye, a resident of Raleigh, North Carolina. His name the board has been unable to learn. (Testimony of Aaron Baer and others.)

The proof of the unparalleled barbarities of the last two men, above mentioned, is very positive and abundant.

The object of this disgraceful sacrifice of human life, in the opinion of the board, perpetrated on the part of the leaders, was to terrify the loyal people of North Carolina, to make them subservient to their foul scheme of rebellion, and to bring contempt upon the government its victims represented, of which the slaughter of the friends and neighbors of these loyal people, the manner in which the bodies of these murdered men were treated, the contempt shown to the persons and property of the widows, also the contemptuous language with reference to the uniform of the United States by General R. F. Hoke, in appealing to the pride and sensibilities of Bryan McCullem, is sufficient evidence; and that they were determined to use these men for this vile purpose is evident from the fact that they were refused either counsel or testimony favorable to them; (testimony of Catherine Summerlin, Mrs. Nancy Jones, Bryan McCullum;) and on the part of those who volunteered to put these men to death, through a spirit of brutish blood-thirst, and a fiendish greed of gain. (Testimony of Aaron Baer and others.) Those directly implicated in the execution of these men were as follows, viz:

The court-martial, of which the board were unable to learn the names of the members; the rebel General Pickett, who ordered the execution; the rebel General R. F. Hoke, who performed the execution; Colonel Baker, who robbed and persecuted their widows; Blunt King, and another voluntary hangman, known as a tall dark-complexioned man, with a cross or squint eye, and a resident of Raleigh, North Carolina.

It is the opinion of the board that these men have violated the rules of war and every principle of humanity, and are guilty of crimes too heinous to be excused by the United States government, and, therefore, that there should be a military commission immediately appointed for the trial of these men, and to inflict upon the perpetrators of such crimes their just punishment.

Trusting this report will meet with your approval, we remain, very respectfully, your obedient servants,

W. H. DOHERTY,
Capt., A. Q. M., and President of Board.
BURTON S. MILLS,
Capt. 14th U. S. C. A., (heavy.)
JONATHAN HOPKINS,
2d Lt. U. S. C. A., (heavy,) and Recorder.

Brevet Major General RUGER, *Raleigh, N. C.*

Official:

W. A. NICHOLS,
Assistant Adjutant General.

No. 4.

NEWBERN, *October* 23, 1865.

The court met in accordance with orders, of which the following is a copy:

[Special Orders, No. 217.—Extract.]

HEADQUARTERS DEPARTMENT OF NORTH CAROLINA,
Raleigh, N. C., October 19, 1865.

7. A board, to consist of the following named officers, is hereby appointed to meet at Newbern, North Carolina, on Monday, October 22, 1865, or as soon thereafter as practicable, to inquire into and report upon the circumstances connected with the alleged murder of a large number of United States soldiers by the rebels during the months of March, April, and May, 1864. The junior member will act as recorder of the court: Captain William H. Doherty, assistant quartermaster; Captain B. S. Mills, 14th United States colored troops; Lieutenant J. Hopkins, 14th United States colored troops.

By order of Brevet Major General Ruger:

J. A. CAMPBELL,
Assistant Adjutant General.

OCTOBER 23, 1865.

Court met in obedience to the above order, all the members—

A number of witnesses were summoned to appear in Newbern, North Carolina, at the office of the provost marshal, on Thursday, the 31st day of October, at ten o'clock a. m., to give evidence in this case.

Court adjourned to said date.

NEWBERN, N. C., *October* 31, 1865.

Court met—all members present—and proceeded to examine witnesses, who testified on oath as follows, viz:

First witness sworn:

Catherine Summerlin, widow of Jesse James Summerlin, testified: That Jesse J. Summerlin, her late husband, resided near Kinston, North Carolina; that he was at the time of his murder by the rebels a soldier enlisted in the service of the United States, in the 2d regiment of North Carolina loyal infantry; that he was taken prisoner by the rebels about the 1st of February, 1864, and hung by them at Kinston, North Carolina, on the 14th or 15th day of the same month; saw her husband (above-named) in the dungeon of the jail at Kinston, North Carolina, on the day before he was executed; was allowed to visit him for a short time on that day and also on the morning of his death; Sheriff Fields was present at the execution; he took the dead body of her husband from the gallows and delivered it to her. The soldiers had stripped the body of all but the pants; she got the body of her husband next morning after execution and carried it home; got a coffin and buried it. Some time afterwards, Colonel Baker, of the rebel army, visited her house, took away her horse and all her provisions; her house was in Jones county, North Carolina; she has 5 (five) small children and is in destitute circumstances. Captain Southeron, of rebel army, was in charge of the prison in Kinston at the time; she was kept under guard (3) three days and nights after the murder of her husband at her own house in Jones county, North Carolina; her husband with (12) twelve others (most of them her neighbors) were hung together from one pole or beam in an old field near the town of Kinston, North Carolina; she was present but dared not look on. She heard the platform fall and saw (4) four or (5) five of the dead bodies, viz: John Brock, Joel Brock, Hardy Dougherty, Stephen Jones, Andrew Britton, and

William Haddock, who gave her his clothes to take to his mother, who was her neighbor. The bodies were stripped in some cases naked all but the shirt or pants. Andrew Britton sent word by her to his wife to meet him in Heaven; her husband was conscripted into the rebel army and carried off by an armed force; therefore, he deserted and came to Newbern and joined the Union forces. She has not yet applied for or received any pension from the United States government.

Second witness sworn:

Mrs. Elizabeth Jones, widow of Stephen Jones, sworn: Her late husband's name was Stephen Jones; she lives in Lenoir county, North Carolina, (1½) one and one half mile from Kinston, North Carolina; her husband volunteered in the rebel home service; in about (12) twelve months was conscripted, then he deserted and came within the Union lines; some time in December, 1863, was taken prisoner by the rebels—same time as Jesse Summerlin; she was in jail in Kinston at the time her husband was imprisoned there, and saw General Hoke.

Court adjourned till 2 o'clock p. m.

Court met 2 o'clock p. m., same day.

Third witness sworn:

Mr. A. M. Daniels sworn: His name is A. M. Daniels; lives in Kinston; is a harness-maker; has been living in Kinston thirteen years; saw some men hung in Kinston; there were (13) thirteen at one time; knows the following that were hung at that time, viz: Wm. O. Haddock, Jesse Summerlin, Wm. Jones, Stephen Jones, Hardy Dougherty, Joseph Brock, John Brock and Andrew Britton; knew these men well; saw them hung with five other citizens; assisted to take down the corpse of Wm. O. Haddock from the gallows, and to bury him; these men assisted in that work were James B. Webb, Daniel Brock and Isaiah Wood. Some of the bodies were buried in the old field outside of town where they were hung. General Pickett was in command of the eastern department of North Carolina at that time, and General Hoke was in command of the post of Kinston, North Carolina; understood those men were tried by a court-martial; saw twenty-three or twenty-four hung at different times; all were executed as deserters from the rebel army. I attended and buried Haddock at the request of his sister, Mrs. Bryant McCullum. J. C. Conner was acting as scout for the rebel army at this time; he took no part in the matter. I knew a man called Blunt King who acted as hangman on one of these occasions, viz: when some United States soldier was hung. Major Nethercutt, of Nethercutt's batallion, was in charge of these men when prisoners. E. C.

Second witness, examination continued: Mrs. E. Jones visited her husband during the two weeks he was kept in prison before his execution—at first in the court-house, at last in the dungeon of the jail; she carried him a bed-quilt to sleep on; visited him the morning he was hung, just before the rebels took him out for execution. On that occasion thirteen were hung together; she received his dead body, carried home and buried it; Major Nethercutt was there at that time. She is poor; has but one child, and no home.

Fourth witness sworn:

Mrs. Nancy Jones, widow of Wm. Jones, sworn: Her late husband's name was Wm. Jones; resides in Lenoir county, North Carolina, (12) twelve miles from Kinston, North Carolina; her husband enlisted in the United States army in January, 1864; was taken prisoner by the rebels in February, 1864; belonged to the same company and regiment in the United States army as the others that were hung at the same time with him; saw her husband in the jail the evening before he was hung, February 14, 1864; could not take her husband home for the want of a conveyance; at first the Union men were afraid to help her, and the rebels cursed her; said it was too good for him. On Wednesday next sent her son, a boy fifteen years old, and her nephew of seventeen years, to bring home the body; they searched a long time and at last found it in an old loft in charge of a sergeant and guard that refused to give it up; at last the doctor gave them it, which was stripped of all covering excepting the socks. This was a week after execution; her son received the body, brought it home and buried it; she was obliged to walk home twelve miles; has five children and no home.

Fifth witness:

Mrs. Celia Jane Brock, widow of John Brock, sworn: Her late husband's name was John C. Brock; he was a soldier in the United States army; enlisted some time in the winter of 1864; he was taken prisoner at Beach Grove, near Newbern, North Carolina, in February, 1864, by the rebel army. She lives four miles from Kinston, North Carolina; saw her husband on the Saturday week before he was executed; he was confined in the dungeon of the jail; he told me that he got only one cracker a day; all the other prisoners said they only got one cracker a day each; she said she fed her husband and the others, or they would have starved. General Hoke was in command then; Captain Kib. Davis was in command at the jail. She took the dead body of her husband home, and buried it. He had been stripped of most of his clothes; her husband was baptized at his own request, on the morning of his execution, by the Rev. Mr. Camp, a baptist preacher of Kinston, North Carolina, in the Neuse river.

Court adjourned to November 1, 1865.

NEWBERN, N. C., *November* 1, 1865.

Court resumed at 10 o'clock a. m.

Sixth witness sworn:

Isaiah Wood sworn: His name is Isaiah Wood; resides in Kinston, North Carolina; jailer of the county jail of Lenoir county; has had that place since and before the war; holds it now; was present at the execution of thirteen United States soldiers in February, 1864, at Kinston, North Carolina; can name the following among them, who were well known to him, viz: Jesse Summerlin, Stephen Jones, William Haddock, John Freeman, Michael Busk, Lewis Freeman, William Irvin, Amos Amyett, and William Brant, also Elijah Killum who was hung afterwards; was jailer at the time, but the military had possession of the jail at the time; knew J. O'Conner, a rebel scout; he was present; witness was present at the hanging of two, (2,) thirteen, (13,) and five (5) United States soldiers at different times; desires now to add to the list of those he saw hung, Andrew Britton, John Stanley, and William D. Jones. A man, called B. King, told witness that he volunteered to hang these men; saw him superintending the execution. The men who were employed by the friends of the hanged men to take up their bodies some time after the execution told him that there were three bodies buried in one grave at the foot of the gallows, and that they could not distinguish them, and they were not removed. Mrs. Irvin sent to the witness requesting him to find out where her son was buried, but he could not do so for the above cause.

Seventh witness sworn:

Mr. Windsor Cook: Lives in Kinston, North Carolina; trade, coachmaker and shoemaker; has lived in Kinston fourteen years; a native of North Carolina; some time in confederate service as guard on railroad; saw thirteen United

States soldiers hung February 15, 1864; knew the following of them: Jesse Summerlin, two Brocks, two Joneses and William Haddock. Major Nethercutt was present.

Eighth witness sworn:

Mr. Daniel S. Brock: Resides in Kinston, North Carolina; agent for the firm of Dibble & Brother, carriage-makers. Witness was present at the execution of United States soldiers at these different occasions: 1st, two men; 2d, thirteen men; 3d, two men were hung; the first two were executed in February, 1864, the last in March, 1864. Witness resides in Kinston; never was in the rebel service; thinks General Hoke was in command; Blunt King was present cutting off the buttons from the clothes of the executed men; he resides in Goldsborough, North Carolina. A stout, tall man with a cross-eye acted as hangman on one occasion; name unknown. Witness gave the names of eighteen United States soldiers he saw hung; (list handed in and kept by recorder of court;) thinks General Hoke was in command at the time at Kinston, North Carolina.

Ninth witness sworn:

Mr. B. W. King: Resides in Kinston, North Carolina; occupation, a farmer; has resided in Kinston thirty-two years; knows of the execution of United States soldiers, but was not present at any of the times; witness helped to bury William Haddock, one of the executed men; saw a number of men, he thinks thirteen, hanging on a gallows, at a distance, but did not go near them, in February, 1864. General Hoke was in command then, and was present at the execution. Witness lives just opposite the jail and court-house; saw these prisoners there; supplied them with food; gave one of them a bed-quilt; thinks they were in charge of Virginia troops; Guilford W. Cox, Pitt county, was provost marshal at the time.

Tenth witness sworn:

Mr. George W. Camp, a merchant and also an ordained preacher of the Baptist church: Saw the execution of thirteen United States soldiers on the 15th of February, 1864. Witness baptized two of them, John and Joel Brock, the morning of the execution in Neuse river; knew some of the hanged men, viz: J. F. Freeman, Jesse Summerlin, Louis Freeman, Hardy Dougherty, and Stephen Jones. General Picket was in command of department of Eastern North Carolina. General Hoke was present in command at Kinston, North Carolina. Major Nethercutt was present; Captain A. Crome, provost marshal; Lieutenant Kib. Davis was acting provost marshal. Witness visited the prisoners in jail twice; heard Sheriff Fields say that he had applied to get off Jesse Summerlin, who had been once his overseer.

Court adjourned.

Court met in Newbern, North Carolina, November 2, 1865.

Eleventh witness sworn:

Mr. J. H. Dibble, merchant and maufacturer: Resided in Kinston, North Carolina, twenty-two years; was there during the rebellion except five or six months, when in prison by the rebels for being a northern man; witness never saw any of the military executions; saw the gallows; knew several of the men hung; knew that the gallows that he saw were erected for the execution of United States soldiers; Captain Wilson was provost marshal then or about that time, also Captain Guilford Cox, Pitt county, North Carolina, also Captain Fry, Onslow county; Generals Picket and Hoke were in command at or near Kinston, North Carolina, and Captain O. S. Dewey was depot quartermaster at that time.

Court adjourned till 2 o'clock p. m.

Court met at 2 o'clock p. m.

Twelfth witness sworn:

Mr. O. S. Dewey: Resides at High Point, North Carolina; formerly post quartermaster in Kinston, North Carolina, for the rebel army, from March, 1862, till March, 1865. He never witnessed any military executions of United States soldiers; remembers the execution of a number of United States soldiers there, in February, 1864, because Captain J. B. Stafford was detailed for the purpose of superintending it, and applied to witness for rope to hang the men with. The witness could not supply him. Rope was at length obtained from the rebel gunboat. General Pickett was in command of department of Eastern North Carolina. Captain Wilson, of the 1st North Carolina rebel sharpshooters, was provost marshal at the time. Witness did not know the men that were hung personally; had no intercourse with them. Captain William C. King was post commissary then at Kinston, North Carolina.

Thirteenth witness sworn:

Mr. C. C. Philips: Resides in Kinston, North Carolina; knows that the following men, United States soldiers in the United States army, were executed there, viz: Mitchel Busick, Louis Freeman, John Freeman, Hardy Dougherty, William Irvin, Joseph Brock, John Brock, Stephen Jones, William Haddock, Jesse Summerlin, Andrew Britton, John Stanely, Louis Bryant, Amos Amyett, David Jones, Maynard Jones. Witness believes the full information can be given by Lieutenant Riggs, formerly of the 2d regiment, North Carolina loyal infantry.

Court adjourned to 10 o'clock to-morrow.

NEWBERN, N. C., *November* 3, 1865.

Court met—all the members present.

Fourteenth witness sworn:

Lieutenant M. S. Riggs: Was a United States soldier of the 1st North Carolina loyal infantry—a lieutenant in company B. Witness knew some of the United States soldiers who were hung at Kinston, in February, 1864, viz: David Jones, Hardy Dougherty, Louis Bryant; thinks that Franklin Bly and Joseph Bly can give information.

Fifteenth witness sworn.

Mr. Joseph Bly: Lives in Newbern, North Carolina; a fisherman; was a soldier in the United States army, in the 1st North Carolina loyal infantry; knows nothing of these men, and can give no information.

Court adjourned to meet at Kinston, North Carolina, in order to obtain more information, and secure the attendance of more witnesses, on the 7th instant.

KINSTON, N. C., *November* 7, 1865.

Court met—all the members present.

Fifteenth witness sworn:

Mr. J. H. Nethercutt: Resides in Jones county, North Carolina; has lived there fourteen years; took a part in the rebellion; held every position in the rebel service, from a private to colonel, nearly; remembers the hanging of a number of United States soldiers in February, 1864; was stationed near Kinston at that time, across the Neuse river; was not present at the execution. Some of the men who were executed had belonged to his command in the confederate service, viz: William Haddock, Louis Taylor, Hardy Dougherty, A. J. Britton, Louis Bryant, M. Busick, Jesse Summerlin, J. C. Brock. These men had volunteered into the battalion of Nethercutt rangers, under promise, from General R. Ransom, rebel mustering officer, that they would not be removed from their homes. They were, however, ordered by the confederate government to be enrolled in the 66th regiment North Carolina troops, by General Clingman, and to report at Goldsborough. About that time, 8th and 13th battalions were thrown together, and constituted the 66th regiment of North Carolina rebel troops. Witness was appointed lieutenant colonel of said regiment, by order of J. J. Selden, the rebel secretary of war. These men, who were thus enrolled, never consented to the change—were greatly dissatisfied with it; never appeared at any muster of said regiment, never answered their names, nor were in any way active members. The men complained that they were unfairly treated. Regiment formed in October, 1863; General Pickett in command of Eastern North Carolina. Witness had no desire for this consolidation; A. D. More was appointed colonel, and witness lieutenant colonel. The men above mentioned, fled to the Union lines, because of these arrangements. No man named Elijah Kellum was at any time under his command. Witness believes that these men were not in sympathy with the rebellion, and wanted to get away from the rebel ranks, using the change of service as a pretext. He believes that A. J. Britton was the leading man in this business; does not know that Britton ever enlisted in the rebel army. Witness was ordered, in February, 1864, by General Hoke, to come to Kinston, North Carolina, and recognize his own men among the prisoners; saw some of the condemned men in the court-house. This was after they had been condemned. Witness asked General Hoke to reprieve these men. Hoke said he had orders to hang them, and would do so. Witness believes the order came from General Pickett, but cannot swear to that fact. Pickett was in command of the department of east North Carolina at the time. Does not know Captain C. S. Toy.

Sixteenth witness sworn:

Mr. William F. Huggins: Resides in Kinston, North Carolina; has lived there from the 1st of 1862; was born in Jones county, North Carolina; saw some United States soldiers on their way to execution in Kinston, North Carolina, February, 1864; knows most of the men, in particular Elijah Kellum, a man of a deformed body and broken constitution. I know that he was never received into any rebel regiment; believe he never was a soldier; no mustering officer would receive him. I know also my own relative, Louis Bryant, who was hung also. Captain R. E. Wilson was provost marshal at the time; he had relieved Croome. E. Kellum was hung after the thirteen who were hung at once. These men were executed at three different times. 1st, two United States soldiers were hung, February, 1864; 2d, thirteen United States soldiers were hung, February, 1864; 3d, seven United States soldiers were hung, February, 1864.

The rebel General Hoke was in command at that time of Kinston, North Carolina.

Seventeenth witness sworn:

Mr. William J. Pope: Resides in Lenoir county, ten miles from Kinston, North Carolina; is provisional sheriff of the county since July, 1865; knows of certain military executions at Kinston, North Carolina, of United States soldiers; was present on one of these occasions; heard General Pickett's order for the hanging of the men read. William Irvin, Hill, and Kellum; thinks they were hung in April; Guttford Cox, provost marshal; Thomas Wilson seemed to superintend.

Court adjourned.

KINSTON, NORTH CAROLINA, *November* 8, 1865.

Court met—all the members present.

Eighteenth witness sworn:

Mr. Aaron Baer: Resides in Kinston, North Carolina; he lived there about sixteen years; a merchant; knows of the execution of United States soldiers; knows that there were, first, 2, then 13, then 7 United States soldiers hung in February and March, 1864. A man named Huggins, who the witness saw in the dungeon of the jail, told him that he had a court-martial. Witness was himself put in the dungeon on the charge of harboring Union men, refugees. Knows Blunt King; heard that he hung the first two. Knows the man that hung the thirteen United States soldiers; he was a tall dark man with a cross-eye. This man stopped at the store of the witness the day of the execution and told him, in a boastful manner, that he had made a good day's work, and was well paid by the clothes of the hanged men, whose he had taken. This man said that he had volunteered to hang them, and would do anything for money. Witness knows that General Hoke was in command at the time; some time afterwards he was arrested by the rebels on the charge of being a Union spy. When under arrest he spoke to General Hoke requesting to be heard in his own defence. Hoke said to him, "Don't speak to me, you damned son of a bitch." The witness made sure of being hung.

Nineteenth witness sworn:

Mr. James B. Wells: Resides in Kinston; has lived there twenty years; a carriage-maker by trade; in 1861 and 1862 he lived in the country, but returned to Kinston in 1863, resided there ever since; knows of the hanging of United States soldiers in the spring of 1864; saw thirteen United States soldiers hung at one time; attended the execution in order to get the body of William Haddock, one of the thirteen hanged men. Saw a man taking off the clothes of the dead bodies; he made an attempt to strip Haddock, but witness prevented him by telling him he had an order for the body from General Hoke. This man was a tall stout man, dark-complexioned, with a cross-eye. Captain Allen Croome was in command of the provost guard, and Captain R. E. Wilson was provost marshal at the time. Witness was present at a meeting of a court-martial that condemned William Haddock; his sister, Mrs. McCullum, requested him to accompany her there, as she was trying to get a summons for a witness to free her brother; all was refused by the court, and neither counsel nor witnesses for the prisoners were admitted. Witness believes that all the thirteen United States soldiers whom he saw hung were condemned by that court.

Twentieth witness sworn:

Mr. William Fields: Resides in Kinston, North Carolina; has lived there for the last twelve years; saw thirteen United States soldiers in February, 1864. Knew personally and well most of them, viz., Mitchel Busick, Amos Amyett, Louis Bryant, J. C. Broek, William Haddock, Jesse Summerlin, William Jones, Louis Freeman, Calvin Hoffman, Stephen Jones, Joseph Broek, Louis Taylor, Charles Catherill, W. Hardy Dougherty, John Freeman, Irvin Hill; saw these men hung. Witness tried to intercede for these men. Did not apply to General Hoke; afraid to do so, yet he is personally afraid of no man; visited these men in prison; assisted to take the bodies down from the gallows for their friends. Thinks John White, of Kinston, North Carolina, was concerned in these executions; thinks John White has run away to avoid the investigation. Joseph Grey can tell all about these executions; he was present at them all. Witness believes that R. E. Wilson, lieutenant in the rebel army, was provost marshal in Kinston, North Carolina, at the time.

Evidence closed.

Twenty-first witness sworn:

Mr. Allen Croome: a farmer; has lived in Kinston, North Carolina, since January, 1864; witness did not see any of the executions of United States soldiers; he was captain of the provost marshal guard, on duty elsewhere; these executions were by the military commander; witness saw the condemned men under guard at the court-house; his appointment was from J. J. Seddon, rebel secretary of war; witness was in Kinston, North Carolina, when the thirteen were hung; thinks Captain Wilson, provost marshal, was not superintending the execution. Understood that there was a court-martial in session at that time, General Picket in command, and General Hoke in command of the post of Kinston; General Carse and some colonel also in command about that time. Captain R. E. Wilson comes from Salem, North Carolina; he did command the post for one day; was provost marshal for several months; I heard rumors that John White of Kingston, North Carolina, volunteered to hang some of these men.

Twenty-second witness sworn:

Mr. S. E. Loften, postmaster in Kinston before and during the war; he saw thirteen United States soldiers hung, in the United States uniform, in Kingston, North Carolina; does not know whether these men were tried by court-martial or not. Does not know who was in command of the post at the time. (Witness seemed reluctant to give any information to the court.)

Court adjourned.

KINSTON, N. C., *November* 9, 1865.

Court met—all the members present.

Twenty-third witness sworn:

Mr. G. W. Cox: Resides in Pitt county, North Carolina; a farmer; he was in the State service of North Carolina during the late rebellion; was captain of the railroad guard of A. and N. C. railroad, to guard the bridges, &c. This company was raised in Pitt county; was commissioned by Henry T. Clark, governor of North Carolina; his company had its headquarters in Kinston, North Carolina; he was made provost marshal of Kinston, North Carolina, in January, 1864; he had been ordered to Virginia with his company; made a written protest against this, but went with his men; they were ordered to be turned over to the camp of instruction or to volunteer into the rebel army; in order to get rid of witness and his perservering complaints of the injustice done to his men the rebel authorities sent him to Kingston, North Carolina, as provost marshal, in October, 1863; he was relieved in February, 1864, but remained a subordinate in the office till April, 1864; Captain R. E. Wilson, who was commanding first battalion of North Carolina troops from Forsythe county, was his successor. Witness knew of the execution of United States soldiers by the rebels; he saw thirteen executed at the same time in February, 1864; these men were in charge of General Pickett's division, provost marshal; they had been turned over to Wilson for safe-keeping and taken from him before the execution; General Hoke was present; General Pickett was near Kinston at the time; knows that there was a court-martial upon those thirteen men; does not know now the names of the members of the court; witness went before the court to bear testimony in favor of Clinton Cox, who was among the prisoners and had been a member of the bridge guard, and who was judged not guilty of desertion, but was detained prisoner by the rebels and died in prison. Knows that the following named men were before the court-martial, viz: John J. Brock and Stephen Jones; does know to what division of rebel army the members of this court-martial belonged; did not hear any application for mercy from any of these men. Thinks the court-martial was from Pickett's division of Virginia troops.

Evidence closed.

Twenty-fourth witness sworn.

Mr. John A. Parrott: Resides three miles from Kinston, North Carolina; a farmer; resided there during the rebellion; never present at any military executions; knew of the hanging of thirteen United States soldiers and assisted to raise the body of one murdered man, (John J. Brock;) Clinton Cox got off from the charge of desertion, but died in a rebel prison; witness knows nothing more of the matter except that there was a court-martial held.

Twenty-fifth witness sworn:

Mr. Bryan McCullum: Resides in Kinston, North Carolina; has lived there sixteen years; keeps a livery stable and blacksmith's shop; was not in the rebel service at any time; knows of the hanging of United States soldiers in Kinston; his wife's brother, Wm. O. Haddock, was hung in February, 1864. The court-martial refused to admit an attorney, or to receive any evidence in favor of the accused. Witness went to General Hoke before the execution, and asked for an order for the body of his brother-in-law in order to bury it. "Hoke inquired if I wanted to bury him in the Yankee uniform? I replied that I did. Hoke then expressed surprise that so respectable a man as I would bury my brother-in-law in Yankee uniform." Captain O. S. Dewy, post quartermaster, who had kindly accompanied me, then interfered and obtained the order for me. I saw General Hoke at his headquarters on the day before the execution of the thirteen United States soldiers.

Court adjourned to meet in Newbern, North Carolina, on the 13th of November, 1865.

NEWBERN, N. C., *November* 13, 1865.

Court met—all present.

Twenty-sixth witness sworn:

Mr. L. S. Baker: Resides in Newbern, North Carolina, since the rebellion; was a brigadier general in the rebel army; was in Florida during the spring of 1864. I know nothing of the execution of United States soldiers in Kinston, North Carolina, in February, 1864, as I was so far away; did not return from Florida till June, 1864. I relieved General Winder, who had been in command at Goldsborough, North Carolina.

Court adjourned.

NOVEMBER 14, 1865.

Twenty-seventh witness sworn:

Lieutenant W. H. Eddings, 14th United States colored troops, heavy artillery: Remembers the time of the execution of the thirteen United States soldiers of the 2d North Carolina loyal infantry by the rebels in Kinston, North Carolina. At that time witness was acting as sergeant major of said regiment and knows that the following men were enlisted and enrolled soldiers in the 2d North Carolina loyal infantry: Joseph Hosket, Mitchel Busick, Amos Amyett, Wm. Haddock, Charles Cutherell, Elijah Kellum, John J. Brock, Andrew J. Britton, Calvin J. Huffman, Joseph Brock, John Freeman, Wm. I. Hill, David Jones, Wm. Irvin, Louis Bryant, Louis Taylor, W. Hardy Doherty, Jesse J. Summerlin, Louis Freeman, Stephen Jones, Wm. Jones, John Stanley.

Court adjourned.

NEWBERN, N. C., *November* 18, 1865.

Court met—all present; and, having read over and revised the notes of the evidence, and approved the report, adjourned *sine die*, directing the recorder to copy and send forward to the commanding general of the department the testimony and report.

W. H. DOHERTY,
Capt. and A. Q. M., President of the Court.

This is a faithful copy of the notes taken in court by the president, and agrees with the notes taken by the recorder more at length.
A true copy:

W. H. DOHERTY,
Capt. and A. Q. M, President of the Court.

Official copy:

WM. ATWOOD,
Assistant Adjutant General,

[Special Orders No. 217.—Extract.]

Proceedings of a court of inquiry convened at Newbern, North Carolina, in obedience to the following order, viz:

HEADQUARTERS DEPARTMENT OF NORTH CAROLINA,
Raleigh, N. C, October 19, 1865.

PARAGRAPH 1. A board, to consist of the following named officers, is hereby appointed to meet at Newbern, North Carolina, on Monday, October 22, 1865, or as soon thereafter as practicable, to inquire into and report upon the circumstances connected with the alleged murder of a large number of United States soldiers by the rebels, during the months of March, April, and May, 1864. The junior member will act as recorder.

Detail for the court.—Captain W. H. Doherty, assistant quartermaster, Captain B. S. Mills, 14th United States colored artillery, (heavy,) Second Lieutenant J. S. Hopkins, 14th United States colored artillery, (heavy.)

By command of Brevet Major General Ruger.

J. A. CAMPBELL,
Assistant Adjutant General.

NEWBERN, N. C., *October 23, 1865.*

The court met pursuant to the foregoing order. Present, Captain B. S. Mills, Captain W. H. Doherty, Lieutenant J. Hopkins.

The court adjourned to meet on Tuesday, October 31, for the purpose of summoning witnesses.

NEWBERN, N. C., *October 31, 1855—10 a. m.*

The court met at 10 a. m., and being duly constituted and sworn, now proceeded to examine witnesses.

Mrs. Catherine Summerlin was called as witness:

Question. Where do you reside?
Answer. In Craven county, North Carolina.
Question. What was your husband's name?
Answer. Jesse James Summerlin.
Question. Was your husband a soldier in the United States army?
Answer. He was an enlisted man in the 2d North Carolina loyal volunteers.
Question. Was your husband ever taken prisoner by the rebels?
Answer. He was.
Question. Where was he taken?
Answer. Near Batchelor's creek, North Carolina.
Question. When was he taken prisoner?
Answer. About the 1st of February, 1864.
Question. When did you see your husband first after his capture?
Answer. At Kinston, North Carolina, in prison, after he was condemned to be hung, on Sunday, as he was hung the next day, Monday.

Question. How long did they allow you to see your husband at a time?

Answer. I saw him twice about three-fourths of an hour, on Sunday, and a quarter of an hour on Monday, the day he was hung.

Question. Did you know any of the rebel officials, and what part did they take with reference to the prisoners?

Answer. I knew a Colonel Baker, who came to my residence while my husband was in prison, and took my horse, and ordered soldiers to take my provisions.

Question. Did you know any one of the men who assisted in hanging your husband?

Answer. I knew Sheriff Fields, who admitted me to the prison, and also took my husband's body from the gallows, and gave his body to me after he was dead. His body was given me the next day after he was executed.

Question. Did you know any other officers?

Answer. One Captain Sutherland also was present, and officiated at the execution. They kept me under guard at my house in Jones county, three days after my husband was executed. My husband was hung at Kinston, in an old field back of the town; I was present but did not see him hung; I could not look at him. I knew he was hung because I received his dead body after he was executed, and heard the scaffold fall from under him. He was hung on the 14th.

Question. Were there any other persons than your husband hung?

Answer. I saw thirteen men, and they were said to have been hung; my feelings would not permit me to see them hanged. I saw six dead bodies that were executed besides my husband. Their names were John Brock, Joel Brock, Hardy Dougherty, Stephen Jones, Andrew Britton, and William Haddock, who gave me his clothes to give to his mother.

Question. Did these bodies have clothes on when you saw them?

Answer. The two Mr. Brocks had; the others were partially stripped, except their under-clothes. Some entirely.

Question. What was done with the dead bodies?

Answer. Their bodies were given to their relatives if called for; the most of them were called for; but the wives of some, within the Union lines, could not get their bodies.

Question. How far do you live from Kinston, North Carolina?

Answer. About twenty miles.

Question. How did you get the body of your husband home?

Answer. William Fields, sheriff, conveyed it there for me.

Question. How many children have you?

Answer. I have five.

Question. Did the rebels take much property from you?

Answer. They took all I had.

Question. Was your husband in the confederate army?

Answer. Yes, he was conscripted.

Question. Do you know what organization of rebel troops he was in?

Answer. The eighth battalion of North Carolina troops.

Question. Was your husband taken into the rebel service by force?

Answer. Yes; there was an armed party came to his house and took him away by force. He afterwards escaped and came to Newbern, North Carolina.

Second witness, Mrs. Stephen Jones, sworn and testified as follows:

Question. What is your name?

Answer. Elizabeth Jones.

Question. What was your husband's name?

Answer. Stephen Jones.

Question. Where do you live?

Answer. About one mile and a half from Kinston, in Lenoir county.
Question. Was your husband ever in the confederate service?
Answer. Yes, he was; he volunteered in that service.
Question. How long was he in that service?
Answer. He was in a number of times, but was sickly and discharged; the last time he was taken by force—conscripted.
Question. Did your husband desert from the rebel service?
Answer. He did, and he came inside the Union lines and enlisted in the Union army.
Question. Do you know when he enlisted in the Union army?
Answer. In December, 1863.
Question. Did you see your husband after he was taken prisoner?
Answer. Yes; I saw him in the court-house and jail at Kinston, North Carolina.
Question. Did you know any of the names of the rebel officers at Kinston?
Answer. I saw General Hoke; I think he was in command at that time.

The court adjourned until 2 p. m., when the third witness, Mr. A. N. Daniels, being sworn, testified as follows:

Question. What is your name?
Answer. A. N. Daniels.
Question. Where do you reside?
Answer. At Kinston, North Carolina.
Question. What is your business?
Answer. A harness-maker.
Question. Where were you born?
Answer. In Connecticut. Am thirteen years a resident of North Carolina.
Question. Did you know any of the men said to have been hung by the rebel authorities?
Answer. A part of them.
Question. Who did you know?
Answer. I knew Wm. O. Haddock, Jesse Summerlin, Wm. Jones, Stephen Jones, Hardy Dougherty, Joseph Brock, John Brock, and Andrew Britton.
Question. Did you see these men hung?
Answer. I did, and assisted in taking down one body after death.
Question. How many did you see hung at this time?
Answer. I saw thirteen.
Question. Did you have anything to do with burying these men?
Answer. One of them, Mr. Wm. O. Haddock, I cut him down and helped bury him.
Question. Who helped you to bury this man?
Answer. Mr. James B. Webb, Daniel Brock, and Isaiah Wood.
Question. How many were buried there?
Answer. Most all; there was only one or two that was given to their friends.
Question. Do you know who was in command of Kinston at that time?
Answer. Hoke was in command of the post, and Pickett in command of eastern North Carolina.
Question. Did you know a man called Colonel Nethercutt?
Answer. I did.
Question. Was he there at this time?
Answer. I did not see him.
Question. Do you know if these men were tried by a court-martial?
Answer. I understood they were.
Question. Do you know any rebel officer presiding at the execution?
Answer. I do not.

Question. Was there any more executions in Kinston besides this that you witnessed?
Answer. Yes; there were some hung before and some after this.
Question. How many did you see hung?
Answer. I saw them all hung—some twenty-three, I think.
Question. What did you understand the charge against them was?
Answer. I understood all were charged with desertion.
Question. Had the man that you buried any family?
Answer. No; his sister, Mrs. Bryan McCullen, requested me to bury him.
Question. Have you ever been in the rebel service?
Answer. Yes; I was in that service eleven months.
Question. Did you know a man by the name of John O'Connor?
Answer. I did.
Question. Was he there at this time?
Answer. He was.
Question. Did he have any part in this?
Answer. I do not think he did.
Question. Do you know a man by the name of Blunt King?
Answer. I do by sight; he acted as hangman at one of the other hangings; cannot say whether before or after.
Question. Do you know the man who acted as hangman on this occasion?
Answer. No; I do not.
Question. Do you know who held these men in confinement?
Answer. I do not know.
Question. How were they treated in confinement?
Answer. I think well, for the neighbors provided for them.

Fourth witness, Mrs. Stephen Jones, recalled and testified as follows:

Question. How long did you see your husband after his capture before he was hung?
Answer. I visited him frequently for two weeks before his death.
Question. Did the authorities treat and provide well for your husband?
Answer. No, they did not; I carried bedding to him myself to keep him from lying on the floor.
Question. Did you make any attempt to intercede for your husband?
Answer. No, I did not; I was told it would be useless.
Question. When did you last see him?
Answer. Monday morning; he was killed that same day.
Question. How many men were executed at the time your husband was?
Answer. Thirteen; I did not see them hung, for I could not stand and see it. I carried my husband's body home with me that same day.
Question. Did you know Major Nethercutt?
Answer. I did; but I do not know whether he had anything to do with them or not. I know he was there, for I saw him in the jail.
Question. Have you a family?
Answer. One child.

Fifth witness, Mrs. Nancy Jones, sworn and testified as follows:

Question. What is your name?
Answer. Nancy Jones.
Question. What was your husband's name?
Answer. William Jones.
Question. Where do you live?
Answer. In Lenoir county, twelve miles from Kinston, North Carolina.
Question. What time did your husband join the Union army?

Answer. He told me that he had enlisted, but I do not know the exact time; some time in January, 1864.

Question. Do you know that he was captured by the rebels, and when?

Answer. Yes; I know he was captured by the rebels some time in the beginning of February, 1864, together with others of the same regiment.

Question. Did you see your husband after he was captured?

Answer. I was allowed to stay one hour with him; it was Sunday morning and he was killed the next day.

Question. Do you know when they were hung?

Answer. On the 15th of February, 1864.

Question. Where was he confined at the last time you saw him?

Answer. In the dungeon of Kinston jail.

Question. Did you get your husband's body after execution?

Answer. Yes; I had him carried home.

Question. Have you a family?

Answer. I have a family of five children.

Question. What condition was your husband's body in when you received it?

Answer. He had nothing on but his socks; I could not take home my husband's body for want of a conveyance. I went home on Wednesday morning, and sent my son, aged 15, and nephew, aged 17, after the body; could get no one else to go. It was a week before I could obtain the body. My son found the body a week after the execution in an old loft, in charge of a guard placed over it by a doctor. The guard refused to let the body go until permission was given by the doctor. Plenty would have been glad to have assisted me, but did not dare to for fear of being called Unionists.

Sixth witness, Mrs. C. J. Brock, sworn and testified as follows:

Question. What is your name?

Answer. Celia Jane Brock.

Question. What was your husband's name?

Answer. John J. Brock.

Question. Was your husband a soldier in the Union army?

Answer. Yes, he was.

Question. When did he join the army?

Answer. I do not know; some time in the winter of 1864.

Question. Was he taken prisoner by the rebels?

Answer. Yes, he was.

Question. When was he taken prisoner, and where?

Answer. Early in the month of February, at Beech Grove, North Carolina.

Question. Where do you live?

Answer. Four miles from Kinston, North Carolina, on the Wilmington road, Lenoir county.

Question. When did you see your husband after being taken prisoner?

Answer. A little over a week before he was killed.

Question. When did you last see your husband alive?

Answer. He went to be baptized on the morning of his execution; I saw him then for the last time alive.

Question. Did you see your husband executed?

Answer. No, I could not look at him being hung.

Question. Did you receive your husband's body?

Answer. Yes, I took his body home that night.

Question. Did they rob his body of clothing?

Answer. He had on nothing but old cast-off clothing.

Question. Who was in command of Kinston at this time?

Answer. General Hoke.

Question. Do you know who had charge of the jail?
Answer. Captain Kit Davis.
Question. Was your husband in the dungeon of the jail?
Answer. Yes; I saw him in there.
Question. How was he treated while in prison?
Answer. Very badly; he told me he had but four crackers to eat in four days. After I got to Kinston he fared better: I then supplied him with food until his death. All the others said the same.
Question. Have you a family?
Answer. I have one child.
Question. Have you any property?
Answer. I have none.
Question. Did you ask any one to let your husband go?
Answer. Yes, but without success.
Adjourned until Wednesday, November 1, at 10 a. m.

WEDNESDAY, *November* 1, 1865—10 a. m.

The court having met, and all being present, then proceeded to examine the seventh witness.

Mr. Isaiah Wood, being sworn, testified as follows:

Question. What is your name?
Answer. Isaiah Wood.
Question. Where do you reside?
Answer. In Kinston, North Carolina.
Question. Were you present at an execution of Union soldiers, at Kinston, North Carolina?
Answer. I was present when thirteen men were hung, and at two other hangings—about twenty in all.
Question. Who were these men that were executed?
Answer. They were captured from the Union army.
Question. Can you tell any of their names, and what are they?
Answer. I can; the names were, Jesse Summerlin, Stephen Jones, Wm. D. Jones, Andrew Britton, John Stanley, Wm. O. Haddock, John Freeman, Elijah Kellum, Mitchel Busick, Louis Freeman, Wm. Irvine, Amos Aymett, and a Mr. Bryan; Kellum was hung after the thirteen.
Question. What was the largest number you ever saw hung at once?
Answer. Thirteen.
Question. Do you know who acted as hangman?
Answer. I did, but have forgotten his name.
Question. When were these men hung?
Answer. Some time in February, 1864.
Question. What is your occupation?
Answer. County jailer, and was before the war; am still in charge of the county jail of Lenoir county, North Carolina.
Question. Were you acquainted with Sheriff Fields, of Kinston, North Carolina?
Answer. Well acquainted.
Question. Did you know one Major Nethercutt?
Answer. I did.
Question. Was he in charge of these men at the time they were hung?
Answer. I cannot say; I do not know whether he was or not.
Question. Do you know whether these men were tried by court-martial or not?
Answer. I do not know.
Question. Did you know a man named John O. Connor?
Answer. I did.
Question. What was his business around Kinston?

Answer. A kind of a scout.
Question. Was he present at the execution?
Answer. I do not know.
Question. How many hangings were there?
Answer. At one time thirteen; at another, five; another, two; and there were some that were shot, but I do not know how many.
Question. How many of these shootings were you present at?
Answer. I was not present at any, but I saw the men taken from the jail?
Question. Do you know Blunt King?
Answer. I did know him.
Question. Did you see him act as hangman at any of these executions?
Answer. Yes; he told me that he volunteered to hang them. It was not at the time the thirteen were hung, but one of the others.
Question. Did you see any of these men buried?
Answer. Yes; I helped bury one; some of them were carried off by their friends; the others were buried at the foot of the gallows.
Question. Did you have anything to do with the others?
Answer. Mrs. Irvine requested me to find her son's body, but I could not find his grave to distinguish it.

Eighth witness sworn, and testified as follows:

Question. What is your name?
Answer. Windsor Coker.
Question. Where do you reside?
Answer. In Kinston.
Question. What is your business?
Answer. Before the war, coach-painting; since then, shoemaker.
Question. How long have you lived in Kinston?
Answer. About fourteen years.
Question. Were you born in the State?
Answer. I was.
Question. Were you there during the war?
Answer. Some of the time I was, and some of the time in the rebel army.
Question. Did you ever know of any military executions in Kinston?
Answer. I saw thirteen men hung.
Question. When was that?
Answer. On the 15th of February, 1864.
Question. Did you know any of the names of the persons who were hung?
Answer. I did; the names were Jesse Summerlin, John Brock, John J. Brock, two Joneses, and Wm. Haddock; that is all I know.
Question. Do you know who was in command of Kinston at this time?
Answer. I did know at the time; I have forgotten.

Ninth witness sworn, and testified as follows:

Question. What is your name?
Answer. Daniel S. Brock.
Question. Where do you reside?
Answer. In Kinston, North Carolina.
Question. What is your business?
Answer. Employed as an agent for the firm of Dibble & Brothers.
Question. Were you present at any military executions at Kinston, North Carolina?
Answer. Yes, at one when two men were hung, one named David Jones; at another a few days afterward when thirteen men were hung; again at another, when two men were hung.
Question. Do you remember the date of the first hanging?

Ex. Doc. 98——3

Answer. No; it was a few days previous to the 15th of February, 1864.
Question. Do you know the date of the third?
Answer. I do not recollect; am under the impression that it was in March. There were four others hung that I was not present at.
Question. Did you reside in Kinston during the war?
Answer. Yes, the whole time, and previous to the war.
Question. Do you know who was in command of Kinston at this time?
Answer. I do not; am under the impression it was General Hoke.
Question. Did you know Major Nethercutt at this time?
Answer. I did, very well; do not know as he had anything to do with this.
Question. Was Blunt King there, and did you know him?
Answer. He was there. I am acquainted with him.
Question. What part did King take in the execution of these men?
Answer. I saw him cutting buttons from the clothes of the bodies.
Question. Can you say whether King acted as an executioner or not?
Answer. Cannot; never saw him do anything but cut buttons from the clothes of the men that were hung.
Question. Where does he reside now?
Answer. In Goldsborough, North Carolina.
Question. Do you know any of these men that were hung, and what were their names?
Answer. Most all of them; I knew the following, and saw them hanged, that I was personally acquainted with: Mitchell Busick, John Freeman, Louis Freeman, Elijah Kellum, Hardy Dougherty, William Irvine, Joseph Broek, John Broek, Stephen Jones, William Jones, William Haddock, Jesse Summerlin, Andrew Britton, John Stanley, Lewis Bryan, Lewis Taylor, Amos Amyett, and David Jones.
Question. Did you know John O'Connor?
Answer. I did; cannot say he was there at any of these executions.
Adjourned until 2 p. m.

Court met pursuant to adjournment. Was then introduced tenth witness, R. W. King, and being duly sworn, testified as follows:
Question. What is your name?
Answer. R. W. King.
Question. Where do you live?
Answer. At Kinston, North Carolina.
Question. What is your occupation?
Answer. A farmer.
Question. How long have you resided in Kinston?
Answer. Thirty-two years.
Question. Did you ever know of any military executions in Kinston?
Answer. Yes, at three different times; I was not present at any; I helped to bury Mr. Wm. Haddock, who was hung there.
Question. Who was in command of Kinston at that time?
Answer. General Hoke. Am under the impression that General Pickett was in command of department at this time.
Question. Did you see the hanging of these men?
Answer. At a distance.
Question. Were these men United States soldiers?
Answer. Yes, they were; they were said to be deserters from the rebel army.
Question. Did you know Major Nethercutt, and was he in town at that time?
Answer. I did know him; do not know whether he was there or not.
Question. Did you see these men while in prison?
Answer. Yes, I did.
Question. Did you know any of these men that were hung?

Answer. Knew most of them.
Question. Did you know what troops were in charge of them?
Answer. I think they were Virginia troops; I think that Guilford W. Cox, Pitt county, was provost marshal at that time. He came inside the Union lines and joined the United States army. Had my farm destroyed by the rebels.
Question. Do you know how these men were treated while in prison?
Answer. I do not; I gave a bed-quilt to one of them.
Question. Did you ever see Blunt King?
Answer. Yes; he was said to have volunteered to hang some of these men.

Eleventh witness sworn, and testified as follows:

Question. What is your name?
Answer. George W. Camp.
Question. Where do you reside?
Answer. In Kinston, North Carolina.
Question. What is your business?
Answer. A merchant, and ordained Baptist preacher.
Question. Did you ever know or see any military executions at Kinston, North Carolina?
Answer. Yes; I was present at an execution of thirteen men.
Question. When was this?
Answer. In February, 1864.
Question. Were these men United States soldiers?
Answer. Yes; they were captured from the United States army.
Question. Did you know these men?
Answer. All by sight, and a few by name.
Question. Did you baptize any of those men before they were hung?
Answer. Yes; two, their names were John and Joseph Brock.
Question. Can you recall any more of these men's names?
Answer. I think there was one Freeman, Summerlin, Jones, Dougherty; there was a pamphlet published in Raleigh, I think, giving all the particulars.
Question. Did you know any of the officers who were in charge at that time?
Answer. Do not; think Hoke was in charge of the vicinity of Kinston, and Pickett in charge of the department.
Question. Did you know Major Nethercutt, and was he present at that time?
Answer. I do; and as far as I recollect, he was present at that time.
Question. Do you know who was provost marshal of Kinston at that time?
Answer. Think Captain Allen Croom; Lieutenant Kit Davis was his assistant provost marshal.
Question. Did you visit these prisoners frequently?
Answer. I visited them twice; they were confined in the old jail.
Question. Do you know how they fared while in prison?
Answer. I do not; it was just previous to their execution I visited them.
Question. Was the man who adjusted the rope a soldier?
Answer. I do not know; think he belonged to some regiment there.
Question. Do you know if an application was made to any one for mercy?
Answer. I think Sheriff Fields did, without success.
Question. Did you hear or know of any one being more bitter than another in pressing this matter forward?
Answer. I did not.
Question. Did you know whether these men were tried by a court-martial or not?
Answer. I did not; I think they were.
Question. Did you attend any of these men at their death?
Answer. I did, one or two, at request of their friends.

Adjourned until 10 a. m. Thursday, November 2, 1865.

THURSDAY, *November* 2, 1865—10 a. m.

Court met pursuant to adjournment; and the twelfth witness, being sworn, testified as follows:

Question. What is your name?
Answer. J. H. Dibble.
Question Where do you live?
Answer. In Kinston, North Carolina.
Question. What is your occupation?
Answer. Carriage manufacturer.
Question. How long have you resided in Kinston, North Carolina?
Answer. About twenty-two years.
Question. Were you there during the rebellion?
Answer. Yes, excepting six months that I was in prison.
Question. By whom were you imprisoned?
Answer. By the confederate authorities.
Question. What were you confined in prison for?
Answer. I do not know, unless it was my northern birth.
Question. Did you ever see any military executions at Kinston, North Carolina?
Answer. I did not; I could see the gallows from my house, but did not go down.
Question. Do you know who was in charge of Kinston at that time?
Answer. Do not; am under impression that Hoke was in charge of the field, and Pickett in charge of the post; they were both there.
Question. Do you know who was sheriff at this time?
Answer. Mr. Fields.
Question. Who was provost marshal?
Answer. Captain Wilson.
Question. Where does he now reside?
Answer. In the western part of the State.
Adjourned until 2 p. m.

Court met pursuant to adjournment; and the thirteenth witness, being sworn, testified as follows:

Question. What is your name?
Answer. O. S. Dewey.
Question. Where do you reside?
Answer. At High Point, North Carolina.
Question. Have you resided in Kinston any part of the past four (4) years?
Answer. Yes, some of the time.
Question. When did you live in Kinston?
Answer. From the 15th of March, 1862, until the 11th of March, 1865.
Question. How were you employed during that time?
Answer. I was post quartermaster in the confederate service.
Question. Were you ever at any military executions in Kinston, North Carolina?
Answer. Yes; I was at the execution of two colored men, shot by order of Colonel Williams, and knew by hearsay that some United States soldiers were hung.
Question. Who was in command of Kinston when these executions took place?
Answer. General Hoke was, and General Pickett in command of the department.
Question. Who was provost marshal of Kinston at that time?
Answer. I think his name was Wilson, captain in 1st North Carolina sharpshooters.

Question. Was Major Nethercutt there at this time?
Answer. Cannot say, although I know the man well.
Question. Who had this execution in charge?
Answer. As far as I can recollect it was a Captain John D. Stafford. The reason it was him, is because he applied to me for rope to hang the men, which I did not have. I think he afterwards got it from a gunboat.
Question. Do you know if these men had a court-martial?
Answer. I do not know.
Question. Did you know these men personally?
Answer. Not one of them.
Question. Who was commissary of subsistence?
Answer. Captain William C. King.
Question. Does he reside there now? (Beaufort, North Carolina.)
Answer. He does at present, I believe.
Question. Do you remember of hearing of other executions besides the thirteen?
Answer. Yes, I have heard of others.

Fourteenth witness was then sworn, and testified as follows:

Question. What is your name?
Answer. C. C. Phillips.
Question. Where do you reside?
Answer. In Kinston at present.
Question. Were you acquainted with any United States soldiers said to have been executed at Kinston by the rebel authorities?
Answer. Yes, I was.
Question. What men do you know, that were United States soldiers, said to have been executed there?
Answer. Mitchell Busick, John Freeman, Louis Freeman, Hardy Dougherty, William Irvine, Joseph Brock, John Brock, Stephen Jones, William Haddock, Jesse J. Summerlin, Andrew Britton, John Stanley, Louis Bryan, Amos Aymett and David Jones.
Adjourned until 10 a. m. Friday, November 3, 1865.

The court met pursuant to adjournment, and the fourteenth witness was sworn, and testified as follows:

Question. What is your name?
Answer. M. L. Riggs.
Question. Were you ever a member of the 2d North Carolina loyal infantry?
Answer. No; I was a member of the 1st North Carolina loyal volunteers.
Question. Were you an officer in that regiment?
Answer. Yes, I was a lieutenant in company B.
Question. Were there ever any of your regiment taken prisoners that were executed?
Answer. I believe not.
Question. Were you ever acquainted with any United States soldiers, said to have been executed at Kinston, North Carolina?
Answer. I was with some.
Question. Name them.
Answer. David Jones, Hardy Dougherty, Lewis Bryan.

Fifteenth witness, Joseph Bly, sworn:

The testimony of this witness not taken, as it was of no use. Adjourned to Kinston, North Carolina, to meet at 10 a. m., Tuesday, November 7, 1865.

KINSTON, N. C., *November* 7, 1865—10 a. m.

The court met pursuant to adjournment, but owing to want of witnesses, adjourned until 2 p. m., when the sixteenth witness was sworn, and testified as follows:

Question. What is your name?
Answer. J. H. Nethercutt.
Question. Where do you reside?
Answer. At present in Jones county, North Carolina.
Question. How long have you resided there?
Answer. Sixteen years next January.
Question. Did you take any part in the late rebellion?
Answer. Yes, I did.
Question. What position did you hold?
Answer. From a private to a colonel, except a non-commissioned officer and second lieutenant.
Question. Were you ever stationed at Kinston, North Carolina, with troops during the rebellion?
Answer. Just across the Neuse river, one mile from Kinston; was once ordered into town for a short time.
Question. Did you ever know of a military execution of United States soldiers in Kinston by the rebels?
Answer. I have heard of it; I was not present at the executions.
Question. Who were the men, and did you know them to be United States soldiers?
Answer. I did not know the men; heard they were United States soldiers.
Question. Did these men ever belong to your command?
Answer. Some of them did.
Question. Did these men ever have a court-martial?
Answer. I do not know.
Question. Could you give the names of any of these men, and what are they?
Answer. I believe there was one Haddock, Taylor, Hardy Dougherty, A. J. Britton, Lewis Bryant, Mitchell Busick, Jesse Summerlin, J. I. Brock.
Question. Do you know whether these men had charges preferred against them?
Answer. I do not know.
Question. What position did you hold at this time?
Answer. Was lieutenant colonel of the 66th North Carolina at that time.
Question. What was this company called that these men belonged to when they first joined the service?
Answer. Partisan Rangers. General Ransom stated to them that probably they would never be removed. This was when the company was first mustered in the service.
Question. What did he mean—never go out the State or locality?
Answer. As I understood it, not out of the locality—by Ransom.
Question. Can you explain what change took place to change them from Rangers to the 66th regiment of North Carolina troops?
Answer. I received an order from General Klingman to report with my command in Goldsborough, North Carolina. As far as I recollect it was the last of July, 1862. When I got to Goldsborough, received orders for two other companies, and mine to be formed in one battalion and elect a major.
Question. What was that battalion called?
Answer. The 8th North Carolina battalion.
Question. What changes took place in order to create the 66th North Carolina regiment?

Answer. The 8th, and I think the 13th battalions were thrown together and then called the 66th North Carolina regiment.

Question. Were you elected major of the 8th battalion, and afterwards appointed as lieutenant colonel of the 66th North Carolina?

Answer. Yes; my commission as lieutenant colonel was signed by Mr. Seddon, rebel secretary of war.

Question. Was it after the consolidation as a regiment that these men deserted?

Answer. As far as I can recollect, these men were never borne on the rolls and returns of the regiment.

Question. How long after forming regiment, before being ordered from vicinity of Kinston and Goldsborough?

Answer. I think it was in October, 1863, before the regiment was formed; the regiment was formed in October.

Question. Were these men allowed to stay about home, while around Kinston?

Answer. Yes, a good deal, for soldiers.

Question. Were you aware of any complaints being made by the men at being formed into a regiment?

Answer. Yes; there was a great deal of dissatisfaction.

Question. Were the men consulted on making this change?

Answer. Not that I am aware of.

Question. Who was in command of Kinston at this time of the execution?

Answer. I do not know; was in Wilmington at that time.

Question. Who was colonel of the 66th North Carolina?

Answer. A. D. Moore.

Question. What do you think caused these men to desert?

Answer. I think all they wanted was an excuse; don't think their sympathies were with the rebellion.

Question. Who do you think the leading man was among them?

Answer. I thought A. J. Britton was ringleader.

Question. Was Elijah Kellum ever enlisted in the rebel army?

Answer. Could not swear that he was; I do not know.

Question. Were you not consulted on the trial of these men?

Answer. I was not.

Question. Did you see any of these men before execution?

Answer. I did; I went to the court-house and saw there those that were condemned.

Question. Do you know how many there were belonging to your regiment?

Answer. I do not recollect now.

Question. Do you know Captain Christopher Foye?

Answer. Yes; I do.

Question. Was he in Kinston at this time?

Answer. I do not know; I think he was.

Question. Did you make any effort to have these men reprieved?

Answer. I asked General Hoke if there could not be something done for them.

Question. What reply did he make?

Answer. He said he could do nothing, as he had an order for their execution.

Question. Who gave this order?

Answer. I cannot swear; I think General Hoke told me it came from General Pickett, in command of Eastern North Carolina.

Question. Did you ever know a Captain Wilson?

Answer. I do not recollect that I did.

Seventeenth witness sworn, and testified as follows:

Question. What is your name?

Answer. W. S. Huggins.

Question. Where do you reside?
Answer. In Kinston, North Carolina.
Question. How long have you resided in Kinston?
Answer. Since the first of 1862.
Question. Are you a native of this State?
Answer. Yes; of Jones county.
Question. Did you ever know of any military executions of United States soldiers in Kinston?
Answer. I saw some on their way to the gallows; I did not witness the hanging.
Question. Did you have any relatives among these men?
Answer. I had one—Mr. Louis Bryan.
Question. Did you know Elijah Kellum?
Answer. Well, I saw him on the way to the gallows.
Question. Do you know whether Elijah Kellum ever volunteered in the rebel service?
Answer. I believe he volunteered in one or two companies; but none of them would receive him, he was so deformed and he had no constitution.
Question. Have you any reason to believe he never was enlisted in the rebel service?
Answer. I have not, only he was so deformed that no medical board would accept him.
Question. Do you know if he was tried and condemned as a deserter?
Answer. I do not; they had some kind of a trial. I never went there, and know nothing about it.
Question. Who was provost marshal in Kinston at this time?
Answer. I think it was R. C. Wilson.
Question. Was Elijah Kellum hung at the time the thirteen were?
Answer. No; it was afterwards.
Question. Do you know how many different executions there were?
Answer. I think there were three; two first, thirteen second, and seven third.
Question. Who was in command of Kinston then?
Answer. General Hoke. This Kellum was to have been sent to conscript camp by some persons who wished to scare him; he hearing of it deserted to the Union lines.

Eighteenth witness sworn, and testified as follows:

Question. What is your name?
Answer. William S. Pope.
Question. Where do you reside?
Answer. In Lenoir county, ten miles from Kinston.
Question. What is your business?
Answer. Provisional sheriff of the county and farmer.
Question. How long have you been sheriff?
Answer. Since first of July, 1865.
Question. Did you hear of any military executions at this post of United States soldiers during the last four years?
Answer. I do.
Question. By whom were the executions performed?
Answer. By the military authorities. General Hoke's brigade marched out with them and hung them.
Question. Who was it had charge of these prisoners?
Answer. I do not know. He was a major; I did not dare to inquire.
Question. Do you know when these men were hung?
Answer. Some time in April, 1864.
Question. Did you hear the order for their execution read?

Answer. I did; it was by order of General Pickett.
Question. Do you know who was provost marshal at this time in Kinston?
Answer. I think it was Captain Guilford Cox; he deserted soon after and went to the Union lines.
Question. Whose evidence hung Kellum?
Answer. Thomas Wilson, of Trenton, North Carolina, conscripting officer.
Adjourned until 10 a. m. Wednesday, November 8, 1865.

NOVEMBER 8, 1865—10 a. m

The court having met pursuant to adjournment, the nineteenth witness was sworn, and testified as follows:
Question. What is your name?
Answer. Aaron Baer.
Question. Where do you reside?
Answer. Here in Kinston.
Question. How long have you resided here?
Answer. Sixteen years.
Question. What is your business?
Answer. A merchant.
Question. Did you ever know of any military executions of United States soldiers in Kinston by the rebels?
Answer. Yes, I did.
Question. Did you witness the execution?
Answer. No, I did not; I did not dare to go.
Question. Do you know if these men had a court-martial?
Answer. One of the prisoners that was not hung told me he was tried by a court-martial. I do not know as the others did.
Question. How many men were executed?
Answer. The first that was hung was two, next seven, and the last thirteen were hung at once.
Question. Did you see any of these men in prison?
Answer. I did not visit them; I did not dare to.
Question. Who was provost marshal at that time?
Answer. I do not know.
Question. Do you know Blunt King?
Answer. I do, personally. He lives in Goldsborough.
Question. Do you know that Blunt King officiated as hangman?
Answer. I understood he acted as volunteer hangman for the first two.
Question. Did you know who volunteered to hang the thirteen.
Answer. A man about six feet high, stout, cross-eyed, told me that he volunteered to hang these men. He stripped the clothes from them the same night he hung them. He told me that he came from Raleigh. He spoke in a boastful way; said he had got well paid for it; that he would do anything for money.
Question. Who was in command of Kinston at this time?
Answer. General Hoke. Hoke had me arrested after this, and before I was put in jail I was carried to the guard-house, and then to the provost marshal's office. While waiting on the piazza I saw General Hoke come out; said "How do you do, general." He said, "don't you speak to me, you d—n—d son of a b—ch."

Twentieth witness sworn, and testified as follows:
Question. What is your name?
Answer. James B. Webb.
Question. Where do you reside?
Answer. In Kinston.
Question. How long have you resided here?

Answer. Some twenty years.
Question. What is your business?
Answer. A carriage-maker.
Question. Did you live here during the rebellion?
Answer. In 1861 and 1862 was living a little way in the country. Moved in the town in 1863.
Question. Did you ever know of any military executions of United States soldiers in Kinston?
Answer. I knew of some that were said to have been United States soldiers.
Question. When did this execution occur?
Answer. Along in the spring of 1864; do not recollect the month.
Question. How many men did you see executed?
Answer. As far as I recollect, I saw thirteen hung at one time.
Question. Were these all you ever saw executed?
Answer. Yes; that was, except some two deserters I saw shot, not United Stated soldiers.
Question. What was your purpose in being at this execution?
Answer. To procure and bury the body of Mr. William O. Haddock.
Question. Did you see any one stripping the bodies of clothing?
Answer. I saw a man stripping several of them. He attempted to take the shoes from the feet of Mr. Haddock while in the coffin. I resisted, and told him I had an order that the body should not be molested.
Question. Describe this man as well as you can.
Answer. He was a tall man, about six feet high; he had a kind of cross-eye, dark complexion, rather stout-built man. Did not know this man's name.
Question. Who was provost marshal at this time?
Answer. I think R. E. Wilson, who commanded the 1st battalion, was.
Question. Did you see this cross-eyed man taking any part in the execution?
Answer. I did not; I stood away from where they were hung, some three hundred yards.
Question. Do you know of any person being more active than another in pushing this execution along?
Answer. I do not.
Question. Do you know whether these men had a court-martial or not?
Answer. I was present at a meeting which I was told was a court-martial, and trying William Haddock. Mrs. Bryan wanted a witness from Wilmington. I went with her to the court.
Question. Who was president of the court?
Answer. I do not know; they were all strangers to me.
Question. Did you understand all of these men were tried by this court?
Answer. I did understand so.

Twenty-first witness sworn, and testified as follows:
Question. What is your name?
Answer. William Fields.
Question. Where do you reside?
Answer. Resided in Kinston for the last twelve years.
Question. Were you here during the late rebellion?
Answer. All the time.
Question. What is your business?
Answer. Sheriff of the county for the last twelve years.
Question. Did you know of any United States soldiers hung in Kinston by the rebel authorities?
Answer. I saw thirteen men hung here in one day.
Question. Did you know their names, and what are they?
Answer. Mitchell Busick, Amos Aymett, Louis Bryan, John J. Brock, Wil-

liam Haddock, Jesse Summerlin, William Jones, Louis Freeman, Calvin Hoffman, Stephen Jones, Joseph Brock, Louis Taylor, Charles Cuthrell, William H. Doherty, John Freeman, Ervin Hill.

Question. Did you make any intercession for these men?
Answer. I certainly did.
Question. Who was it that you applied to for mercy?
Answer. I do not know the man's name; did not apply to the general.
Question. Who executed these men?
Answer. Do not know; think it was John White, from on board the rebel ram. He ran away from Kinston on this account, I believe.
Question. Who was provost marshal of Kinston, at this time?
Answer. Do not know; I think it was R. E. Wilson.
Adjourned until 2 o'clock p. m.

The court having met pursuant to adjournment, the twenty-second witness was sworn, and testified as follows:
Question. What is your name?
Answer. Allen Croom.
Question. Where do you reside?
Answer. In Kinston.
Question. What is your occupation?
Answer. Farmer.
Question. How long have you resided here?
Answer. Since January, 1864.
Question. Has there ever been any military execution of United States soldiers, to your knowledge?
Answer. I never witnessed; I have heard, by report, that there was. I knew these men in jail, dressed in United States uniform, said to be deserters from the rebel army. I saw them in confinement at the court-house.
Question. What were you doing at that time?
Answer. I was in charge of a provost guard in this place.
Question. By whom were you appointed a captain of provost guard?
Answer. Received my commission from Mr. Seddon, rebel secretary of war.
Question. Were you in town when thirteen men were said to have been executed?
Answer. I was.
Question. What was this company called that you was in command of?
Answer. Kinston provost guard.
Question. Who was provost marshal at this time?
Answer. Captain R. E. Wilson.
Question. Do you know, were these men executed under Wilson's direction?
Answer. I do not know. I think he was about the office.
Question. Did you know any of the men that were hung?
Answer. I knew one—William Jones.
Question. Did these men ever have a court-martial.
Answer. I do not know. I knew there was a court-martial in session at that time.
Question. Do you know who was in command of the post of Kinston at that time?
Answer. I do not know; am not positive whether General Hoke was or not; think that same week, General Hoke, General Corse, a colonel, and Captain Davis, were all in command.
Question. Did you ever hear of any person coming from Raleigh or Goldsborough to hang these men?
Answer. I do not, to my recollection.

Question. Did you hear anything about one John White volunteering to do it?
Answer. Not at that time. Since then I have heard that he did.

Twenty-third witness sworn, and testified as follows:
Question. What is your name?
Answer. S. E. Lofton.
Question. Where do you reside?
Answer. Here, in Kinston.
Question. What is your occupation?
Answer. Postmaster at Kinston.
Question. Were you ever engaged in the late rebellion?
Answer. Only in keeping post office.
Question. Did you know of any United States soldiers being hung at Kinston?
Answer. I saw thirteen men hung there, said to have been United States soldiers.
Question. When did this take place?
Answer. I cannot say when or what time.
Question. Do you know if these men were tried by a court-martial?
Answer. I do not.
Question. Who executed these men?
Answer. I do not know; they were all strangers to me.
Question. Did you hear of any one robbing these men, or participating in the execution?
Answer. I had heard of such taking place, but did not know of any one.
Adjourned until 10 a. m., Thursday, November 9, 1865.

NOVEMBER 9—10 a. m.

The court met pursuant to adjournment.
Twenty-fourth witness sworn, and testified as follows:
Question. What is your name?
Answer. Guilford W. Cox.
Question. Where do you reside?
Answer. In Pitt county, North Carolina.
Question. What is your occupation?
Answer. A farmer.
Question. Did you take any part in the late rebellion?
Answer. I was captain of a company in the local service.
Question. Where was this company raised, and what was it called?
Answer. In Pitt and Lenior counties; they were called Atlantic and North Carolina Railroad Bridge Guard.
Question. Were you ever commissioned as captain of this company?
Answer. I was, by Governor Clark, of North Carolina.
Question. Where was this company stationed?
Answer. On the bridges of the Atlantic and North Carolina railroad.
Question. Where were your headquarters?
Answer. Principally at Kinston, North Carolina.
Question. Were you ever provost marshal of Kinston, North Carolina?
Answer. I was ordered in May, 1863, to proceed with my company to Virginia. I at first refused; but afterwards, at the solicitation of my men, went under protest. Was kept there until October, 1863; when, on account of the annoyance I gave, was ordered with my command to Kinston, North Carolina, myself as provost marshal, and my men to be given the choice between volunteering for general service or be sent to the conscription camp. This was in

MURDER OF UNION SOLDIERS IN NORTH CAROLINA.   45

October, 1863. Was relieved of the provost marshalship about the 14th of February, 1863.

Question. Who signed this order?
Answer. Mr Seddon, rebel secretary of war.
Question. How long did you act as provost marshal?
Answer. From October, 1863, to middle of February, 1864.
Question. Who relieved you as provost marshal?
Answer. Captain R. E. Wilson, of Forsyth county, commanding 1st North Carolina batallion.
Question. Did you know of any execution of United States soldiers by rebel authorities?
Answer. Yes, I did.
Question. What time did you witness these executions?
Answer. I saw thirteen executed in February, 1864. That is all I was witness to.
Question. Who was provost marshal at that time?
Answer. R. E. Wilson. These men were in charge of General Pickett's division, provost marshal. He turned them over to Wilson for safe-keeping until further orders; but before execution, were turned back to Pickett's provost marshal.
Question. Was Pickett here at that time?
Answer. He was here about that time.
Question. Was Hoke here at that time?
Answer. Yes, he was. He was brigadier general at that time.
Question. Did you know a tall, cross-eyed person who acted as hangman?
Answer. I do not.
Question. Do you know if there was a court-martial?
Answer. I do know there was; I had myself summoned in the case of Clinton Cox. The court asked me if he ever belonged to my company; my answer was yes; and asked me if he deserted; I told them no, for I did not consider desertion from a local company desertion from rebel service.
Question. Do you know any of the members of this court?
Answer. I do not.
Question. Do you know if any of these men were tried by that court-martial?
Answer. Yes; I know John J. Brock and Stephen Jones were; knew them personally.
Question. Do you know to what division the officers composing the court belonged?
Answer. I do not; think it was Hoke's division.
Question. Did you hear of any application having been made for mercy for these men?
Answer. I did not.
Question. Did you see Hoke there?
Answer. I do not remember.

Twenty-fifth witness examined, and testified as follows:

Question. What is your name?
Answer. John A. Parrott.
Question. Where do you live?
Answer. Three miles from Kinston.
Question. What is your occupation?
Answer. A farmer.
Question. Have you resided here during the rebellion?
Answer. Nearly all the time.
Answer. Did you know of any execution taking place in Kinston, of United States soldiers?

Answer. Was not witness to any; have heard there was; could hear the music at the time thirteen men were executed.

Question. Did you ever have anything to do with burying any one said to have been hung?

Answer. I helped carry one from his temporary grave.

Question. What was his name?

Answer. John J. Brock.

Question. Who pointed them out as deserters?

Answer. I don't remember now who did.

Question. Did any one ask you to designate any one of these men?

Answer. I don't think there was.

Question. Where were these men when you saw them?

Answer. I saw them near the corner of the court-house. I pointed out one man, Clinton Cox, to Judge Manly, who stood near me, and told him that was the man that broke out of Salisbury jail; merely to hear what he would say.

Question. Was Clinton Cox executed?

Answer. He was not; he died in prison.

Question. Was Clinton Cox tried before a court-martial?

Answer. I think he was; I do not know.

Question. Did you ever tell anybody that Cox never was a rebel soldier?

Answer. I do not recollect that I ever did.

Question. Why was Cox not executed?

Answer. The only reason was, I believe, that he had been exchanged from a rebel prison as a Union soldier. He was imprisoned at Salisbury as a Union sympathizer, and had his choice given him of joining on either side; he chose the Union side; and I think that was the reason he was not hung. That is what I have understood.

Question. What became of Clinton Cox?

Answer. He died in prison.

Adjourned until 2 p. m.

Twenty-sixth witness was sworn, and testified as follows:

Question. What is your name?

Answer. Bryan McCallan.

Question. Where do you live?

Answer. In Kinston.

Question. How long have you lived here?

Answer. Sixteen years.

Question. What is your business?

Answer. Livery stable keeper and blacksmith.

Question. Were you engaged in the late rebellion?

Answer. I was not.

Question. Did you know of the execution of United States soldiers at Kinston by rebel authorities?

Answer. Yes; I had a brother-in-law hung, Wm. O. Haddock.

Question. Did you make any intercession for your brother to any one?

Answer. I procured an attorney to bring forward evidence in favor of him, but the court-martial would not admit him.

Question. Did you have any conversation with General Hoke?

Answer. I went to General Hoke for an order to get Wm. Haddock's body, and he asked me if I wanted my wife's brother buried in a Yankee uniform; I told him I wanted him buried just as he came from the gallows, and he said he did not think that a man of my standing would want him buried in that uniform. Captain O. S. Dewey interfered, and procured the order.

Question. Did you ever hear the name of the hangman?
Answer. I did not.

Adjourned to meet at Newbern, North Carolina, on Monday, November 13, 1865.

NEWBERN, NORTH CAROLINA,
November 13, 1865—10 a. m.

The court having met, pursuant to adjournment, the twenty-seventh witness, Mr. L. S. Baker, was sworn; but as it appears from his testimony he knew nothing about the case, adjourned until 10 a. m., November 14, 1865.

The court met pursuant to adjournment, and the twenty-eighth witness was sworn, and testified as follows:

Question. What is your name?
Answer. Wm. H. Eddins.
Question. Where is your residence?
Answer. Have none at present; am an officer in the United States army.
Question. What regiment and what rank?
Answer. Fourteenth United States colored artillery, (heavy,) first lieutenant and adjutant.
Question. Were you ever a member of the second North Carolina loyal volunteers?
Answer. I was acting sergeant major.
Question. Do you know the following named men to have been enlisted men in that regiment, viz: Joseph L. Hasket, David Jones, Mitchell Busick, Wm. Irvine, Amos Aymett, Lewis Bryan, John J. Brock, Wm. Haddock, Jesse J. Summerlin, Andrew J. Britton, Lewis Freeman, Calvin J. Hoffman, Stephen Jones, Joseph Brock, Lewis Taylor, Chas. Cuthrell, Wm. H. Dougherty, and Elijah Kellum?
Answer. I know these men to have been enlisted in the second North Carolina loyal volunteers.

I certify that the foregoing testimony is correct as taken by the board.

JONATHAN HOPKINS,
2d Lt. 14th U. S. C. Art'y, (heavy,) Recorder of the Court.

Official:

W. A. NICHOLS,
Assistant Adjutant General.

No. 6.

BUREAU OF MILITARY JUSTICE,
War Department, December 12, 1865.

A memorial and other papers relating to the barbarous slaying upon the gallows of certain Union soldiers, by so-called military authority at Kinston, North Carolina, in the spring of 1864, are respectfully returned to the Secretary of War for the President.

Under date of September 13, 1865, Captain W. H. Doherty, assistant quartermaster, addressed to Brevet Major General Ruger, commanding department of North Carolina, a memorial, setting forth that twenty-two United States soldiers, belonging to the 1st and 2d North Carolina loyal infantry, captured by rebel forces under the command of Generals Pickett and Hoke, in the month of February, 1864, were deliberately murdered by public hanging at Kinston, North Carolina, in that and the succeeding month, under circumstances of great cruelty and barbarity, and by authority of said Pickett and Hoke, under the false charge that they were traitors and deserters. The memorial contains the names of a portion of the murdered men, and of active rebels supposed to have been implicated in their murder. It also furnishes the names of several persons supposed to be able to testify in relation to the matter, and asked that a military commission should be appointed by the commanding general, with full power to investigate the murderous outrage and bring the guilty to punishment. This memorial being submitted to the Secretary of War on the 11th of November, 1865, was referred back to General Ruger for report. Under date of November 25 General Ruger forwards the report of a board of inquiry convened by his order at Newbern, North Carolina, October 22, 1865, of which Captain Doherty, the memorialist, was president, accompanied with the record of its proceedings. After setting forth the characteristic barbarities practiced upon the prisoners by their inhuman captors while in prison, and the revolting circumstances of savage cruelty attending their execution, as shown by the record, the report goes on to state, "that although these men were arraigned and tried as deserters, the testimony of Colonel Nethercutt proves conclusively that they belonged to the local North Carolina service, and that they never had been confederate soldiers; therefore, in the opinion of the board, a confederate States court-martial had no jurisdiction over them. And further, the court-martial virtually acknowledged its incapacity in the case of Clinton Cox, who was arraigned upon the same charge, but who was saved from the fate of the others by the testimony of the captain of a local North Carolina company, to the effect that, in leaving his company without authority, Cox did not, in his opinion, become a deserter from the confederate service." The board, therefore, recommend the immediate appointment of a military commission for the trial of the parties implicated, especially General Pickett, who ordered the execution; General Hoke, who was in charge of it; the members of the court-martial who sentenced them, whose names are unknown; a Colonel Baker, who robbed and persecuted their families; and two volunteer executioners, one of whom is Blunt King, residing at Goldsborough; the other, whose name is unknown, but of whom a minute personal description is given, residing at Raleigh. It would appear from the record that the board of inquiry misapprehended the effect of Nethercutt's testimony in regard to the status of these murdered men in the rebel service; and that although he testified in respect to seven of them, who were in his command, that they were originally mustered into the service as members of a company of partisan rangers, and were told by General Ramsom that they probably would not be ordered away from the neighborhood of their homes, he further stated that they were subsequently, under his, Nethercutt's, command, ordered to Goldsborough, and there incorporated with the 66th North Carolina, in the confederate service, its officers being commissioned by the confederate government.

The record furnishes no evidence that the unhappy victims of this outrage were not deserters, so far as an abandonment of a constrained and hated service would warrant their being stigmatized as such; but, on the contrary, the little evidence on that point furnished by the record tends to show that they were. The two first witnesses who testified before the board were widows of two of these victims; each declared that her husband had deserted after being conscripted into the rebel service, and one declared that her husband had previously volunteered, and been discharged for disability. No question was put to any other witness on this point. In respect, however, to the monstrous barbarity and guilt involved in the execution of these Union soldiers, it is of little consequence whether or not they had, before entering into the service of the United States, fled from the despotic servitude of a rebel conscription. It appears from the testimony relating to Clinton Cox, referred to in the report of the board of inquiry as having escaped condemnation with the other victims because the company from which he deserted was a local one, organized by the State of North Carolina, that, subsequent to his desertion in October, 1863, the choice was given that company either to volunteer for the general confederate service, or be sent to the conscript camp; and it was well understood throughout the country at the time that, in 1863–'64, the whole serviceable population of the south was swept into the rebel army by a most ruthless conscription demanding a service that was treason against all their obligations as American citizens. Submission to that service was, in itself, a crime from which it was their bounden duty, as men and as patriots, to flee at the first opportunity. Having so fled and taken service and shelter under their country's flag, they were entitled to the protection of that country so long as it could be extended to them, and to its ample vengeance upon their oppressors and murderers for their shameful death, inflicted, as it was, under circumstances of contumely and ferocious cruelty rarely equalled by savages.

While it is the opinion of this office that every sentiment of patriotism and public justice forbids that the blood of these murdered men should cry in vain from their dishonored graves for vengeance, it finds in the evidence submitted to it no grounds upon which personal charges could be established and sustained against the guilty parties. There was no evidence before the court of inquiry showing conclusively by whom or by whose order these sufferers were arrested and prosecuted; by whom tried, condemned, or executed. It is recommended, therefore, by this office, that the papers in the case be returned to the commanding general of the department of North Carolina, with instructions to cause further and minute investigations to be made into the circumstances of the case, with the view of tracing and fixing the guilt of its lawless and savage transactions upon individuals who can be held responsible for them; collecting testimony that will be likely to establish such guilt. And, in case the investigation shall prove successful, to prepare charges against such parties, and forthwith appoint a military commission for their trial.

J. HOLT,
Judge Advocate General.

The SECRETARY OF WAR.

The memorial of Captain W. H. Doherty, assistant quartermaster of Newbern, North Carolina, respectfully showeth: That the undersigned, moved by a sincere desire to vindicate the honor and maintain the authority of the United States government, and to bring to justice certain wicked and cruel men who have deliberately murdered, by public hanging, a number of loyal citizens and soldiers of the United States, when prisoners, during the late rebellion, desires to call the attention of the general in command to the following facts; and, on the part of the widows and orphans of our murdered soldiers, and of the outraged laws of our country and of humanity, respectfully solicits a thorough investigation of these atrocious crimes.

That after the capture by the rebel forces under Generals Pickett and Hoke, in the month of February, 1864, at Beach Grove, near Newbern, North Carolina, of some companies of the 1st and 2d North Carolina loyal infantry volunteers, United States troops, it can be proved that twenty-two (22) soldiers of these regiments were hung at Kinston, North Carolina, on the false charges of being traitors and deserters, whereas, in truth, they were brave United States soldiers, fighting under the protection of the flag of their country, and in the uniform of the United States volunteers. That these men were executed under circumstances of brutal cruelty and wanton insult. Thirteen of them were hanged nearly or altogether naked, from one beam or pole, at the same time, in the public square or street of Kinston, North Carolina, and left to writhe and struggle till dead. That the rebel Generals Pickett and Hoke, and Lieutenant Colonel John Nethercutt, of the 66th North Carolina rebel regiment, and many others of the slaveholding aristocracy of North Carolina, are responsible for

Ex. Doc. 98——4

this odious cruelty. That the following are the names of some of the victims, all good and true United States soldiers at the time of their murder, viz:

Jesse Summerell, 2d North Carolina; Hardy Dougherty, 2d North Carolina; Stephen Jones, 2d North Carolina; David Jones, 2d North Carolina; William Haddock, 2d North Carolina; John Freeman, 2d North Carolina; John Brock, 2d North Carolina; Charles Cutherall, 2d North Carolina; —— Kellum, 2d North Carolina; Mitchel Busick, 2d North Carolina; Louis Freeman, 2d North Carolina; Joseph Haskett, 2d North Carolina; William Irvine, 2d North Carolina; Amos Aymett, 2d North Carolina.

That these poor men were all hanged from the same pole, in violation of all law, merely because of their devotion to the Union cause, in Kinston, North Carolina, in March, 1864.

Also, a few days afterwards, ten (10) more soldiers of the same regiment, whose names are not yet ascertained, were hung at the same place by the same rebel generals.

That again, soon after the capture of Plymouth, North Carolina, by the rebel forces under Hoke, on the 20th day of April, 1864, Sergeant Joseph Fulcher, of the 2d North Carolina loyal infantry, was shot after being taken prisoner, at Halifax, North Carolina, and Privates Stephen H. Jones, William D. Jones, and John J. Brock, of the same regiment, were hung at Kinston, North Carolina, in April or May, 1864.

That the widows of some of these men are alive, and able and willing to give valuable evidence in the matter, viz:

Mrs. Catharine Summerell, Mrs. Nancy Jones, Mrs. Stephen Jones, Mrs. Sally Brock, Mrs. —— Freeman, and others.

And the following were present at these executions, and should be called upon as witnesses: Henry Strong, attorney; William Field, sheriff; Reverend Geo. W. Camp, preacher; also Mr. J. H. Dibble, a loyal Union man, and Winger Cooker.

That the following are said to be implicated in this cruelty:

William Field, sheriff; Shadrach E. Loftin, Elijah F. Loftin, Captain William Sutten, James W. Morris, esq., Major John G. Wooten, Preacher —— Cooval, Wiat Churchwell.

That the undersigned believes this to have been the most cruel and brutal action of the whole rebellion, a flagrant insult to the United States government, intended to terrify and subdue the poor whites of North Carolina, who were mostly Union men, and to compel them to fight against their country. That, therefore, he requests, respectfully, that a military commission be appointed by the commanding general, with full power to investigate this matter, and to expose the cruelty, vindicate the law, and punish the guilty, and restore the dignity of the United States government which has been violated by this monstrous outrage.

Respectfully submitted:

W. H. DOHERTY,
Captain and Assistant Quartermaster.

Brevet Major General RUGER,
   Commanding Department of North Carolina.
Official:

W. A. NICHOLS,
Assistant Adjutant General.

NEWBERN, N. C., *September* 13, 1865.

STATE OF NORTH CAROLINA, EXECUTIVE DEPARTMENT,
Raleigh, N. C., November 23, 1865.

COLONEL: Your communication to the governor of yesterday's date, making inquiry relative to the organizations of State troops in this State during the late rebellion, is to hand, and I have the honor, in answer, to state that there were two classes of troops belonging to and retained by the State during the rebellion, to wit: "North Carolina State troops," about twenty-two hundred (2,200) in number, consisting of a battalion of artillery commanded by Major Alexander McRoe, one regiment of infantry commanded by Colonel James W. Hinton, one battalion of infantry commanded by Lieutenant Colonel Whitford, and two or three detached companies in eastern North Carolina, kept regularly in service, paid, clothed, and subsisted by the State, (except when temporarily under the command of so-called confederate general officers,) and took no oath except allegiance to the State authorities. These were entirely under the command of the governor of the State and subject to no other authority except by his order, temporarily. He could not transfer them. The other class was the entire militia of the State consolidated into an organization called "a guard for home defence." These, by the act of the legislature, consisted of every white male person not enrolled in confederate service, between eighteen and fifty years, except the executive, judicial, and legislative departments of the State, and were liable to be called into active service by the governor for a term not exceeding ninety (90) days, not to go beyond the limits of the State and not qualified by oath at all. They were not transferable to any other authority.

I have the honor to be, very respectfully, your obedient servant,
EUGENE GRISSOM, *Aide-de-Camp.*

Colonel J. A. CAMPBELL,
Assistant Adjutant General U. S. A., Raleigh, N. C.

STATE OF NORTH CAROLINA, EXECUTIVE DEPARTMENT,
Raleigh, N. C., January 27, 1866.

GENERAL: A gentleman applied to me this morning who represented himself as a member of a court or board of inquiry, desiring certain information, to wit: "proceedings of courts-martial during the war of 1863-4;" "correspondence between the executive department and confederate authorities respecting the execution of alleged deserters;" "orders issuing from military department appertaining to trial and execution of alleged deserters."

No adjutant general has yet been appointed by the State. The papers belonging to the military department of the State during the war are boxed up in the office of the secretary of state here, and may be inspected by any person you may appoint, and every facility I can afford will be given; but I learn from a young man who was in the office of the adjutant general throughout the war, that no trial of any alleged deserter occurred during the war under any State court-martial; and he further states that no orders were issued in relation to the trial and execution of deserters. These trials and executions, as he avers, were all made under the orders of the confederate authorities.

"The correspondence between the executive department and the confederate authorities, respecting the execution of alleged deserters," if any such exists, is in the hands of the United States authorities, having been captured by the military on the occupation of this city and sent, as I am informed, to Washington city.

Very respectfully, your obedient servant,
W. H.

Brevet Major General T. H. RUGER,
Commanding Department of North Carolina.

HEADQUARTERS DEPARTMENT OF NORTH CAROLINA,
Raleigh, N. C., April 18, 1866.

GENERAL: I have the honor to acknowledge the receipt of telegram of this date, directing me to return papers connected with the hanging of certain North Carolina United States prisoners, by direction of Hoke and Pickett, late rebel generals, at Kinston, North Carolina, in April or May, 1864, referred to me December 15, 1865, and to report what steps I have taken in the matter. The papers in the matter are herewith respectfully forwarded. No steps have been taken by me other than those necessary to ascertain the truth of the matter.

A board of officers was detailed by me on January 17, 1866, to further investigate the matter. Such board of officers, after such investigation as could be had, made report herewith forwarded. The information obtained by said board not being sufficiently full to enable me to act with confidence in the matter as directed, I wrote on yesterday a letter addressed to yourself asking that I be furnished with a copy of the court-martial proceedings had by the rebel military authorities in the case of the United States prisoners executed at Kinston, North Carolina, if such proceedings could be found among the rebel archives. The matter has been delayed, owing to the difficulty of obtaining evidence of persons having knowledge of the facts.

Very respectfully, your obedient servant,
THOS. H. RUGER,
Brevet Major General Vols., Commanding.
Brevet Major General E. D. TOWNSEND,
Assistant Adjutant General, U. S. A., Washington, D. C.

HEADQUARTERS DEPARTMENT OF NORTH CAROLINA,
Raleigh, N. C., November 25, 1865.

GENERAL: In reply to the indorsement of the honorable Secretary of War on the memorial of Captain W. H. Doherty, assistant quartermaster volunteers, (returned herewith,) I have the honor to forward herewith the report of a board convened by my order on the receipt of the original memorial of Captain Doherty, to investigate and report upon the circumstances connected with the alleged murders.

I also forward letter from an aide-de-camp of Governor Holden in reply to a letter from these headquarters, making inquiries as to the status of the North Carolina State troops, to which organization it would seem, from the evidence, that some of the men executed by the rebel authorities had at one time belonged.

I have the honor to be, general, very respectfully, your obedient servant,
THOS. H. RUGER,
Brevet Major General Vols., Commanding.
Brigadier General E. D. TOWNSEND,
Assistant Adjutant General. Washington, D. C.

THIRTY-NINTH CONGRESS, FIRST SESSION.

CONGRESS OF THE UNITED STATES,
In the House of Representatives, April 16, 1866.

On motion of Mr. Schenck,

Resolved, That the Secretary of War be directed to communicate to this house a report of the Judge Advocate General, and such other information as may be of record or on file in his department on the subject, which will show what are the facts in the case, and what steps have been taken to bring to

MURDER OF UNION SOLDIERS IN NORTH CAROLINA.

justice and punishment the murderers of the following named Union soldiers, belonging to the first and second regiments of North Carolina loyal infantry, alleged to have been tried and executed by orders of the rebel Generals Pickett and Hoke, under the pretext of their being deserters from the confederate service, viz: Jesse Summerell, Hardy Dougherty, Stephen Jones, David Jones, William Haddock, John Freeman, John Brock, Sergeant Joseph Fulcher, William D. Jones, Charles Cutherall, ——— Kellum, Mitchell Busick, Louis Freeman, Joseph Haskett, William Irvine, Amos Aymett, Stephen H. Jones, J. J. Brock.

Attest:

Official:

EDWARD McPHERSON, *Clerk.*

W. A. NICHOLS,
Assistant Adjutant General.

No. 7.

BUREAU OF MILITARY JUSTICE,
War Department, December 30, 1865.

An examination of a memorial and other papers submitted to it, relating to the barbarous slaying upon the gallows of certain unarmed Union soldiers, by so-called military authority of rebel forces, at Kinston, North Carolina, in the spring of 1864, led this office to report, under date of 13th instant, that while in its opinion every sentiment of patriotism and public justice forbids that the blood of these murdered men should cry in vain from their dishonored graves for vengeance, it found in the evidence submitted to it no grounds upon which personal charges could be established and sustained against the guilty parties. It therefore recommended that the papers in the case be returned to the commanding general of the department of North Carolina, with instructions to cause further and minute investigation to be made into the circumstances attending this outrage, with the view of tracing and fixing its guilt upon individuals who can be held responsible; and in case the investigation should prove successful, to prepare charges against such parties, and forthwith appoint a military commission for their trial. There was no evidence in the papers then under consideration showing conclusively by whom, or by whose order, these sufferers were arrested, condemned, or slain; but a letter of inquiry addressed by this office to General Peck, then commanding in North Carolina, led him to refer to a correspondence held by him with General Pickett, of the rebel army, in February, 1864. It will be seen from copies of this correspondence, which is submitted herewith, that the letters of General Pickett of 16th and 17th February supply, to a large extent, the deficiency of evidence referred to. Not only does the imperious and vaunting temper in which these letters are written indicate his readiness to commit this or any kindred atrocity, but his boastful admissions that he was in command at the time, that the twenty-two men, of whose names he furnishes a list, had been executed, and his threat that he would retaliate in the proportion of ten to one by executions among the 450 officers and men, whom he says "I have in my hands, and subject to my order," all tend to show that he was in responsible command, and furnish evidence upon which it is believed charges can be sustained against him.

It is therefore recommended that these additional papers be transmitted to the general commanding, to be used in connexion with such other evidence as may result from the investigation now in progress; and when the preparation of the case shall have been completed, charges be preferred against the said G.

E. Pickett, and such other persons as may be shown to have been in complicity with him in these murders, and their trial ordered. As a preliminary step to such trial it is suggested that Pickett be at once arrested and held to await it, upon the evidence furnished in his correspondence adverted to, which is deemed abundantly sufficient to warrant such arrest.

                 J. HOLT,
                 Judge Advocate General.

The SECRETARY OF WAR.

Official copy:

                 WM. ATWOOD,
                 Assistant Adjutant General.

No. 8.

           SYRACUSE, NEW YORK, *December* 22, 1865.

GENERAL: I have the honor to acknowledge the receipt of yours of the 18th instant, in relation to my correspondence while commanding the "army of North Carolina," with the rebel General George E. Pickett, touching the execution of twenty-two United States soldiers in the winter of 1864, as alleged deserters from the rebel army.

Deeming the matter a grave one, I promptly advised the department of my action. April 13, 1864, I transmitted for the honorable Secretary of War, from the headquarters of the army of North Carolina an official copy of this correspondence with both lists.

It is proper to state that General Pickett published in the rebel papers a letter purporting to be an answer to my final communication of February 27, but which he never transmitted to me or my successor.

The correspondence thus transmitted will fully explain the circumstances under which I addressed General Pickett, and give the status of the fifty-three North Carolinians, for whom I demanded the treatment due prisoners of war.

As requested, I enclose the original communication of Major General George E. Pickett, from "Headquarters Department of North Carolina, Petersburg, Virginia, February 17, 1864," with his "list of prisoners" captured before Newbern and executed at Kinston, North Carolina, as deserters from the confederate army.

Any aid or assistance in my power will be cheerfully given you at any time.

I remain, general, most respectfully, your obedient servant,

                 JOHN PECK,
                 Late Major General U. S. A.

GENERAL J. HOLT,
 Judge Advocate General, Washington.

Official copy:

                 WM. ATWOOD,
                 Ass't Adj't. General.

Respectfully referred to the Judge Advocate General United States army.
                 E. D. TOWNSEND,
                 Assistant Adjutant General.

ADJUTANT GENERAL'S OFFICE,
 December 29, 1865.

No. 9.

WAR DEPARTMENT, BUREAU OF MILITARY JUSTICE,
Washington, D. C., December 30, 1865.

SIR: Referring to our conversation this morning in regard to the rebel General Pickett, I beg to submit the enclosed copy of a letter addressed by him to General Peck, the original of which is in my hands. Were this paper referred to the Attorney General, it is thought that its temper and avowals might assist in determining the question of the writer's pardon, which is said to be pending before the President. I shall recommend the arrest and trial of Pickett for the murder of the twenty-two Union prisoners of war who were executed under his authority.

Very respectfully, your obedient servant.

J. HOLT,
Judge Adrocate General.

Hon. E. M. STANTON, *Secretary of War.*

Official copy:
WM. ATWOOD,
Ass't Adj't General.

No. 10.

Report of a board of inquiry, convened per Special Order No. 15, *dated headquarters department of North Carolina, Raleigh, North Carolina, January* 17, 1866, *"to inquire into and report upon the circumstances connected with the alleged murder of a number of United States soldiers by the rebels, during the months of March, April, and May,* 1864, *and to fix the guilt of their murders on individuals who can be held responsible."*

RALEIGH, N. C., *March* 29, 1866.

In pursuance of the above mentioned order, the board met at Raleigh, North Carolina, January 23, 1866, and proceeded to examine the papers submitted by the adjutant general of the department for its information and guidance.

Under these it was discovered that a previous board had sat upon this same investigation; the board did not, therefore, consider it necessary to examine again the witnesses whose testimony had already been taken.

Great difficulty was experienced in finding any new evidence which might reasonably bear upon "the circumstances of the murder, and to fix the guilt upon individuals."

Great distaste was quite generally exhibited by the witnesses to testify, lest they might be considered by their friends in the light of "informers." Defective memories seemed to be prevalent in reference to occurrences at the particular times specified—the witnesses alleging, however, with some show of reason, that the exciting military events then constantly succeeding each other unremittedly did not permit these particular ones to make deep impressions.

The members of the board, at different times, visited Salisbury, Goldsborough, Kinston, Newbern, Halifax, Beaufort, and other localities, for the purpose of making minute inquiries; they made personal inquiries of members of the State legislature, the secretary of state, the governor of the State, ex-Provisional Governor Holden, and whoever they thought might be likely to afford information.

With the permission of the governor of the State, the records of the State adjutant general's office, contained in many large boxes, were examined to find, if possible, the "muster in" or other muster-rolls of the particular troops to which these men were alleged to have belonged in the rebel service, as it was understood that such rolls contained the statement of the specific service which local troops were enlisted to perform; also to ascertain whether any court-martial proceedings were there filed, under which these men were judged and deprived of their lives.

Nothing, however, was found, although the court-martial records and regimental muster-roll of most of the North Carolina troops were found.

It is regretted that no return has been received to the communication forwarded to the custodian of the rebel archives at Washington, January 26, 1866, for the obtaining of such documentary evidence there filed as would have, in some measure, elucidated this investigation.

From the evidence adduced it would seem that all those captured from the United States forces in the advance of the rebels on Newbern, in February, 1864, and executed, had previously been enlisted either in the military service of the so-called Confederate States for general or "local" service, or in Whitford's battalion (67th North Carolina regiment) of State troops. (*Vide* testimony of Quartermaster John Hughes, and testimony of Lieutenant Colonel S. McD. Tate.)

The charges appear in each case to have been "desertion," and pretty generally the same, though (*vide* testimony of Lieutenant Colonel Tate) some were alleged in the charges "to have been in arms against the Confederate States," and others "to have been found at Batchelor's Creek with United States uniforms on."

The testimony taken by this board is direct that Joseph Hasket and David Jones, who were among those first tried and executed at Kinston, had previously been enlisted men in the 10th North Carolina rebel artillery for "general" service.

The State of North Carolina organized regiments for "general" service which, after organization, were duly turned over to the so-called confederate government. These were the North Carolina troops "for the war" or definite periods, and the State lost all control of their movements after the transfer.

In addition to these, the State organized for "local defence," under a special State statute, certain regiments, viz: the 67th and 68th regiments, and the 69th battalion, generally termed "partisan rangers," which were exclusively State troops, paid, clothed, and subsisted by the State, and for its especial defence. These troops could not be removed form the State. They were, however, with the sanction of the rebel State authorities, almost always "acting under the orders of the confederate generals commanding the districts in which they were located."

To this class of "local defence" troops some few of those captured from the Union forces, and executed, seem to have belonged; and from the evidence it is apparent that at the time of these executions, the 67th regiment of State troops (Whitford's battalion) was acting in conjunction with the confederate forces, and under the orders of the confederate Major General G. E. Pickett.

Aside from these two classes of troops, the so-called confederate congress passed an act August 21, 1861, "to provide for local defence and special service," whereby certain kinds of volunteer forces were organized for specific purposes, and with certain privileges. Their muster-rolls specified they were raised under this act, and setting forth distinctly the services to be performed. They were not considered as in actual service, for the purpose of receiving pay and subsistence, except when called out by the rebel president. They were not to be called out until a necessity arose for their services, and should not be required to go beyond the limits of the State to which they belonged. They were expected to serve when called out only so long as the emergency existed, and then return to their ordinary pursuits until again called.

This, in brief, comprised the "terms of enlistment" of this class of confederate troops, and under this head were organized various "bridge guard companies" and "local defence battalions."

The evidence shows that the 8th battalion of the North Carolina troops, commonly called "Nethercutt's battalion," or "partisan rangers," commanded by Major J. H. Nethercutt, was one of these confederate local defence battalions, organized by the confederate government for "local defence service." To this battalion the testimony of the former board of inquiry evidences that seven of those hung had previously been enlisted in prior to joining the United States army.

The evidence shows that this class of troops were found to be of little or no service; that men volunteered therein for the purpose of being out of danger, avoiding conscription, and remaining near their homes—a feeling which caused little sympathy for them among the rank and file of the rebel army.

The sweeping conscription act, and the necessity for men, induced the rebel war department, as is shown by the testimony, to attempt to consolidate their "local defence" organizations into regiments, and send them to the "front." Thus Nethercutt's and Wright's battalions and some "bridge guard" companies were assembled and ordered up to Kinston from the localities in which they were respectively serving, and, in obedience to orders for the consolidation from the rebel war department at Richmond, an order was issued by the district commander, Brigadier General J. G. Martin, for their consolidation into a regiment denominated afterwards the 66th North Carolina, and to which A. D. Moore was appointed colonel by the rebel president.

It is shown that this consolidation was distasteful to Nethercutt's men, and that considering it was violating the terms of their enlistment, many took to the woods and deserted, and coming into the Union lines, enlisted in the 2d North Carolina loyal volunteers.

That (*vide* testimony of Lieutenant Snow, A. D. C.) at first not half of Nethercutt's battalion came up for consolidation, and that an extraordinary camp guard was required around them after the consolidation into the 66th regiment.

That (*vide* testimony of Lieutenant Justice, A. D. C.) Major General G. E. Pickett afterwards issued a proclamation requiring these deserters to come in and surrender themselves, and that some did, and were sent to the regiment at Wilmington.

It is likewise evidenced that most of these men were within the conscriptive ages of the then recent sweeping conscription law.

That the so-called confederate government considered it would be a violation of the terms of their enlistment in the confederate local defence service to transfer them *bodily* to the 66th regiment for *general* service, and therefore gave them the chance either to go willingly, or else be discharged from their battalion and be conscripted on the spot into the 66th.

It seems, however, (*vide* testimony of General Martin,) that Nethercutt's battalion, as an organization, *was* transferred *bodily* to the 66th, as most of the men were liable for conscription under the conscript law by reason of age, and claimed by the rebel war department. That the confederate authorities, in executing the conscript law, had no authority to act upon "local service organizations as such," but simply upon individuals whose age and condition made them liable. That most went into the 66th, of Nethercutt's men, rather than go to the conscript camp, as many desertions occurred when the regiment was ordered from Kinston to Wilmington.

As the rebel assistant adjutant general of the State at that time testifies, the offer of discharge and conscription was merely a change on paper—the individual was held all the same, and "restrained of his liberty."

It is to be regretted that the board could not ascertain more definitely as to whether the names of those executed were ever borne on the rolls of the 66th as "volunteers," or whether they deserted before consolidation.

The testimony of Judge Battel, of the North Carolina supreme court, clearly shows, that many petitions for the writ of habeas corpus being presented to him he discharged the petitioners from military custody on the ground, "that having enlisted for particular *special* service, they could not be conscripted for the *general* service, but *could* be held for the *special* service they had originally enlisted for, and which they were still liable to perform.

How far the so-called confederate government had the belligerent right to discharge its enlisted men of these local defence battalions from service, and conscript them on the spot for *general* service on refusal to enter voluntarily into the 66th, this board did not feel called upon to determine.

It is proven that the 66th regiment, composed of these "local service" battalions, afterwards was sent from the limits of North Carolina to the rebel army of Virginia.

The testimony of General Martin, in whose brigade the 66th was, and under whose direction the consolidation was completed, is to the effect that "an enlisted man would not have violated the terms of enlistment in Nethercutt's battalion by going home instead of to the 66th regiment, but that he would have been treated as a deserter under the rebel conscript law, and the orders issued in pursuance thereof."

He also says, that at the times of the executions in 1864 he was told by some of the officers of Nethercutt's battalion in the 66th "that some of their men had just been shot at Kinston for desertion."

The evidence all tends to prove indirectly that a general court-martial was held at Kinston by the rebels for the trial of all our captured Union soldiers who were executed; that they were alleged to have been deserters from the rebel service; that the usual proceedings were gone through with customary at military executions, such as troops, parades under arms, and courts-martial proceedings and orders read by officers of the general staff, &c. It is also proven that Major General G. E. Pickett was in command of the rebel forces at the times of these various executions of captured Union soldiers at Kinston; that he gave the orders for their execution, and that no other officer in the rebel department of Eastern North Carolina had authority to order an execution but him.

The testimony of Blunt King, of Goldsborough, hangman at one of these executions, is interesting as showing the "animus" of the commanding rebel general. Irrelevant evidence induces the board to give full credence to King's testimony, despite the rather unfavorable character attributed to him by the inquiry of the previous board.

The correspondence between Major General John Peck, commanding United States forces in North Carolina, and Major General G. E. Pickett, (copies of which are appended to the evidence,) tends in some degree to elucidate this inquiry.

Files of such newspaper journals of the State (to the number of 11) for 1863-'64 as could be obtained, were examined by the board; and such as contained any allusions to these murders are also appended to the testimony.

As to the guilt of individuals concerned in the execution of the United States soldiers captured on the Newbern expedition and who had previously taken voluntary service and been duly enlisted in the rebel army, either in the 10th North Carolina artillery for general service, or in the 67th North Carolina regiment (Whitford's battalion) State troops for *local* service, the board refrain from reporting, as under the belligerent rights at that time accorded the rebels, there would seem to be but little doubt as to the "jus bellæ" inherent to belligerency to punish desertion capitally.

As to the execution, however, by the rebels of such Union soldiers from the 2d North Carolina loyal volunteers as had, previous to enlisting in our service, either deserted from Nethercutt's local defence battalion or the bridge guard companies, upon the attempt to consolidate into the 66th, or deserted after such consolidation, or, being loyal North Carolinians, had fled from conscription service, before or after their conscription, the board have been guided by the opinion of the Judge Advocate General of the 12th December, 1865, on the investigation of the previous board.

That opinion upon the case of the local company to which Clinton Cox belonged, and which was given the choice to enlist or be conscripted into the rebel service, declares:

"'That it was well understood throughout the country that in 1863-'64 the whole serviceable population of the south was swept into the rebel army by a most ruthless conscription, demanding a service that was treason against all their obligations as American citizens. Submission to that service was in itself a crime, from which it was their bounden duty as men and patriots to flee at the first opportunity. Having so fled and taken service and shelter under their country's flag, they were entitled to the protection of that country so long as it could be extended to them, and to its ample vengeance upon their oppressors and murderers for their shameful death."

The board are therefore of the opinion that the rebel Major General G. E. Pickett, commanding the department of eastern North Carolina, in 1864, in the language of the Judge Advocate General, "was the guilty party by whom or by whose order these sufferers were arrested and prosecuted, and by whose order executed."

The board regret their inability, after diligent search, to prove "by whom these men were tried and condemned."

The evidence taken tends towards showing that the court-martial before which they were brought was a general court-martial ordered by General Pickett, composed principally of Virginians, although there seems to have been more than one court in session at the same time.

While other prominent rebels seem to have been concerned in these shameful transactions as accessories, the evidence clearly shows that General Pickett was the prominent authority under whose direction everything connected with the murder of our soldiers took place; and the board are therefore unable, from the evidence they have been able to collect, to fix the guilt upon any subordinate in such a manner as to contain grounds sufficient for preferring personal charges.

All of which is respectfully submitted.

        ASA BIRD GARDNER,
   1st Lieut. and Adj't 7th Reg't V. R. C., and
      President Board of Inquiry.
      GEORGE H. PENNIMAN,
  1st Lieut. 28th Mich. Inf. Vols., and Recorder.
      WILLIAM R. WILCOX,
    2d Lieut. Co. K, 28th Mich. Inf. Vols.

Brevet Major General T. H. RUGER,
 Commanding Dep't of North Carolina, Raleigh, N. C.

[Special Order No. 15.—Extract.]

HEADQUARTERS DEPARTMENT OF NORTH CAROLINA,
Raleigh, North Carolina, January 17, 1866.

* * * * * * *

A board of officers is hereby appointed to convene at Raleigh, North Carolina, on the 23d day of January, 1866, or as soon thereafter as practicable, to inquire into and report upon the circumstances connected with the alleged murder of a number of United States soldiers by the rebels during the months of March, April, and May, 1864, and to fix the guilt of these murders on individuals who can be held responsible.

The board will proceed from time to time to such places in the department as may be necessary to procure and establish the facts in the case.

Detailed for the board, 1st Lieutenant and Adjutant Asa Bird Gardner, 7th regiment, Veteran Reserve Corps; 1st Lieutenant George H. Penniman, 28th Michigan volunteer infantry; 2d lieutenant William R. Wilcox, 28th Michigan volunteer infantry. Lieutenant Penniman will act as recorder of the board.

By command of Brevet Major General Ruger:

J. A. CAMPBELL,
Assistant Adjutant General.

A true copy:

ASA BIRD GARDNER,
1st Lieut. and Adj't 7th Reg't V. R. C., and
President Board of Inquiry.

Official:
W. A. NICHOLS,
Assistant Adjutant General.

No. 11.

Abstract of testimony, taken before the board of inquiry convened per Special Order No. 15, headquarters department of North Carolina, Raleigh, January 17, 1866, in the matter of the murder of certain Union soldiers at Kinston, by the rebels, in 1864.

Proceedings of a board of inquiry convened at Raleigh, North Carolina, by virtue of the following order, viz:

[Special Order No. 15.—Extract.]

HEADQUARTERS DEPARTMENT OF NORTH CAROLINA,
Raleigh, North Carolina, January 17, 1866.

* * * * * * *

A board of officers is hereby appointed to convene at Raleigh, North Carolina, on the 23d day of January, 1866, or as soon thereafter as practicable, to inquire into and report upon the circumstances connected with the alleged murder of a number of United States soldiers by the rebels during the months of March, April, and May, 1864, and to fix the guilt of these murders on individuals who can be held responsible.

The board will proceed from time to time to such places in the department as may be necessary to procure and establish the facts in the case.

Detailed for the board, 1st Lieutenant and Adjutant Asa Bird Gardner, 7th regiment Veteran Reserve Corps; 1st Lieutenant George H. Penniman, 28th Michigan volunteer infantry; 2d Lieutenant William R. Wilcox, 28th Michigan volunteer infantry. Lieutenant Penniman will act as recorder of the board.

By command of Brevet Major General Ruger:

J. A. CAMPBELL,
Assistant Adjutant General.

A true copy:

ASA BIRD GARDNER,
1st Lieut. and Adj't 7th Reg't V. R. C., and
President Board of Inquiry.

TUESDAY, *January* 23, 1866.

The court met in pursuance of the above order at department headquarters, Raleigh, North Carolina, at 10 o'clock a. m., all the members being present, and having duly organized under oath, according to the articles of war in such cases made and provided, adjourned to the 24th day of January, 1866, in order to peruse papers submitted for examination.

JANUARY 24, 1866.

Court met pursuant to adjournment at 10 o'clock a. m., all the members being present. After consultation it was considered advisable that the recorder should wait upon the governor of the State, in order to ascertain the whereabouts of records of proceedings of courts-martial or orders and proceedings of rebel authorities of the State of North Carolina, or of the so-called Confederate States, during the years 1863 and 1864, respecting matters under investigation; also to confer with ex-Provisional Governor Holden and others, to make proper inquiries respecting the execution of certain alleged deserters at Kinston, North Carolina, by the rebel authorities of the so-called Confederate States. Adjourned to the 25th day of January, 1866, at 10 o'clock a. m.

JANUARY 25, 1866.

The court met pursuant to adjournment, all the members being present. After hearing the report of the recorder respecting the interview with Governor Worth. ex-Provisional Governor Holden, and others, the court directed the recorder to summon witnesses familiar with the transactions in the adjutant general's office of North Carolina, through department headquarters, to the officer in charge of rebel archives at Washington, D. C., requesting search to be made for proceedings or records of proceedings calculated to throw light upon the subject-matter of investigation, and adjourned until the 26th day of January, 1866, at 10 o'clock a. m.

JANUARY 27, 1866.

The court met in pursuance of adjournment, all the members being present. Private Adonijah N. Proctor, company K, 28th Michigan volunteers, reported as clerk in compliance with the detail. After consultation the court adjourned, for the purpose of awaiting the attendance of witnesses, to the 29th day of January, 1866, at 10 o'clock a. m.

JANUARY 29, 1866.

The court met in pursuance of adjournment, all the members being present. In consequence of the non-attendance of witnesses, after consultation the board adjourned until the 30th day of January, at 10 o'clock a. m., for the purpose of examining records and papers by the secretary of state of the State of North Carolina, January 30, 1866, at 10 o'clock a. m.

JANUARY, 30, 1866.

The court met in pursuance of adjournment, all the members being present

First witness, John B. Neathery, being duly sworn by the recorder, deposed as follows:

Question. What is your name and age?
Answer. My name is John B. Neathery, and am thirty years of age.
Question. Where do you reside, and what is your occupation?
Answer. I reside in Raleigh, and am a printer.
Question. What was your occupation in 1864?
Answer. I was an assistant adjutant general in 1863 and 1864, in the office of the adjutant general of North Carolina, at Raleigh, North Carolina, with the rank of first lieutenant.
Question. What was the nature of your duties?
Answer. My business was divided in totwo departments, "military" and "troops." I attended troops department, but attended military department in

1864, there being no other clerk. There was a correspondence kept up in the State. A. M. McPheeters, clerk to Governor Vance, living in Raleigh.

Question. Do you know what officer was in command at Kinston, North Carolina, when certain alleged deserters were executed in the early part of 1864?

Answer. General G. E. Pickett was in command in the department, including Kinston, at that time. I was in Kinston a few days after the execution in April, and recollect the people expressed great regret at the execution, feeling that it was for a small offence. I had a conversation with Mr. Higgins, who was in Kinston and witnessed the execution. I frequently issued orders to regiments in State service (67th and 68th) for court-martials. They were sometimes called "partisan rangers;" the 69th was a State battalion. These troops remained in State service till the surrender. They drew their pay and clothing from the State, but were rationed by the confederate government. There were some "partisan rangers" raised under confederate authority, and possibly some muster-rolls came to the State. The 66th was formed of these, and also Nethercutt's battalion. As "partisan rangers," they could not be removed from their immediate section. When they were found to be of little use, an order was issued for their transfer to the 66th regiment. The order was considered a violation of the terms of their enlistment, and opposed to by the men. The men were given their choice of going into the 66th regiment or being mustered out and conscripted, which amounted to the same thing.

Question. State your sum of information respecting the status of the North Carolina State militia, or what you know about proceedings of court-martials in the year 1864?

Answer. I frequently issued orders to regiments in State service (67th and 68th) for court-martials. They were sometimes called "partisan rangers;" the 69th was a State battalion. These troops remained in the State service till the surrender. They drew their pay and clothing from the State, but were rationed by the confederate government. There were some "partisan rangers" raised under confederate authority, and possibly some muster-rolls came to the State. The 66th was formed of Nethercutt's battalion. As "partisan rangers," they could not be removed out of their immediate section. When they were found to be of little use, an order was issued for their transfer to the 66th regiment. The order was considered a violation of the terms of their enlistment, and ojected to by the men. They were given their choice of going into the 66th regiment or being mustered out and conscripted, which amounted to the same thing—"whipping the devil around the stump." It was understood by the confederate authorities to be a violation of their organized enlistment; it was considered merely a change of position on paper, as they would have been sent to the regiment all the same under the confederate conscript laws. This order was from the Confederate States; I think there was some objection by the State authorities, the general opinion being that by entering the local defence service one escaped being sent to Virginia. It was understood that men enlisted in these organizations to avoid being removed from their section to more active service. The dissatisfaction of the State was evinced by a protest. Many of these men transferred to the 66th without their consent were discharged by *habeas corpus* by the supreme court of the State. The troops were enlisted under act of the State, and then transferred to Confederate States. These "partisan rangers" were enrolled under confederate act, generally remained at home, being out, say, a week at a time on what was called scouts. They had no regular camp, and some would always be at home. I think they drew rations from the confederate authorities, and were supposed to be in camp. They were required to make reports; it was a loose arrangement; the officers sympathized with the men, and but few reports were made. There was a local militia also, composed of militia officers, magistrates, &c., though none except those who were necessary to execute the laws of the State, as the governor determined. Sometimes there were forty militia officers in a county and no enlisted men.

Question. Do you know the name of the officer commanding this department in 1864?

Answer. General Pickett was in command in North Carolina. I think the "partisan rangers," as an organization, was abolished in the latter part of 1863; it was considered one of the most perfect ways to avoid conscription, to enlist in an organization for "local defence," similar to the "partisan rangers." I never heard of any men being arrested after being discharged on writs of *habeas corpus;* the writ directed them to be sent to their homes and there remain unmolested. The writ was suspended in this State on that account. Judge Battle discharged some from the 66th. I remember one company of which he discharged two men. The legality of the order transferring them was declared null and void, but that these men were liable to duty under the original act, under which they had enlisted. I know of but little more of the "partisan rangers;" some were discharged under writs of *habeas corpus;* some were dragooned into the service, and others succeeded in effecting their escape to the woods. My impression is that they were not allowed to return to their homes; the pressure was for men, and they were compelled to consent to go into the 66th, or to be discharged and conscripted on the spot into the regiment; the whole thing was on paper, and ultimately meant service in the 66th any way. The 66th was a collection of odds and ends not belonging to any other organizations, by officers who had seen service, and thought they deserved places. In nearly all the regiments the officers were allowed to elect their field officers, but in this regiment the field officers were appointed by the confederate government, without consent of the line officers, and not chosen from them, except Major J. H. Nethercutt. There were four companies of partisan rangers, and four bridge guards.

The court then adjourned until 10 o'clock a. m., February 1, 1866.

FEBRUARY 1, 1866.

The court met in pursuance of adjournment, all the members being present. Minutes of last meeting read and approved. The president reported that the boxes containing the books and papers of the confederate adjutant general had been partially examined, and was in hopes that the roll and papers containing evidence of the court-martials could be found. The recorder was instructed to summon the clerk of the supreme court and George Snow to appear as witnesses before this court on to-morrow. The court then adjourned until 10 o'clock a. m., February 2, 1866.

FEBRUARY 2, 1866.

The court convened at 10 o'clok a. m. in pursuance of adjournment, all the members present.

Second witness, Edmund B. Freeman, being duly sworn, testified as follows:

Question. What is your name, age, and residence?

Answer. My name is Edmund B. Freeman; age, seventy; residence, Raleigh, since 1833. Have been engaged during the whole time as clerk of the supreme court of North Carolina.

Question. Have you had charge of the files of the records in the office for the past five years?

Answer. Yes, perfect control of them. Judge Richmond M. Pierson was chief justice of North Carolina in 1864, and Judges Battle and Manly were the associate justices.

Question. What was the practice of court at chambers, generally, as to filing written decisions?

Answer. The court hears decisions as to *habeas corpus* cases at chambers, and returns the written decision to the superior court clerk's office in the county petitioner resides.

Question. Was it customary to file on record in the clerk's office any decision of a justice at chambers?

Answer. No, sir; unless removed there by writ of *certiorari*.

Question. Was the decision of the judge of the supreme court in these *habeas corpus* cases final?

Answer. Yes, sir; the petition was either overruled or granted.

Question. Was it the practice of the justice to keep the record of proceedings?

Answer. No, sir, not usually; they were published in the newspapers.

Question. Was it your custom to notice the decisions generally made by the judges at chambers?

Answer. No, sir; only as papers came before me as clerk.

Question. Do you remember any *habeas corpus* cases before Judge Battle early in 1864?

Answer. No, sir; I believe there were none in this county.

Question. Can you not call to mind the nature of any *habeas corpus* decisions made early in 1864?

Answer. No, sir; there was no one I was interested in.

Question. Was it not your custom to read over the petition?

Answer. No, sir; only ask the petitioner if he has read over the petition, and then swore him to it as commissioner.

Question. Do you not recollect of hearing of certain prisoners held under military authority being discharged by one or more justices of the supreme court early in 1864 or late in 1863?

Answer. No, sir, I do not; my memory is not good at best.

Question. From whom did you receive your appointment as clerk?

Answer. By the court.

Question. Are these reports correct copies of decisions made in the supreme court?

Answer. They are.

Question. Who was reporter of the decisions of the supreme court in 1863 and 1864?

Answer. Patrick Winston.

Third witness, George Snow, being duly sworn, testified as follows:

Question. What is your name, residence, and occupation?

Answer. George Snow; age, 19; residence, Raleigh, always; occupation, running a saw-mill.

Question. What was your occupation in 1863 and 1864?

Answer. I was in the army a part of 1863 and all of 1864.

Question. What capacity?

Answer. First as aide-de-camp to Brigadier General Martin, with rank of lieutenant.

Question. What department was General Martin's brigade in?

Answer. Department of east North Carolina, with headquarters at Kinston.

Question. Where were you stationed in January, February, March, and April, 1864?

Answer. At Nassau, Bermuda, part of the time; but in field was in Virginia.

Question. With whom did you go to Bermuda?

Answer. With Captain Crossman as captain's clerk, though still in the service. It was a sort of leave of absence. I went with permission of General Martin and the department general.

Question. Were you ever aide-de-camp for anybody else?

Answer. Yes; Colonel Cowans, in A. P. Hill's corps. I was on his staff one month.

Question. What regiments composed his brigade?

Answer. The 7th, 18th, 28th, 33d, and 37th North Carolina.

Question. How long were you in North Carolina during January, February, March, and April, 1864?

Answer. About ten days; I came from Wilmington, North Carolina.

Question. What division commander did you serve under in 1863 and 1864?

Answer. Major General Whiting at Wilmington, commanding department; Major General Wilcox, who was my immediate commander in 3d army corps of A. P. Hill.

Question. Did you ever hear of Major General Pickett?

Answer. Yes, sir; have seen him.

Question. Did you ever serve under him?

Answer. I do not know whether General Martin was ever subject to his orders when in North Carolina; not otherwise.

Question. What was your regiment?

Answer. 33d North Carolina.

Question. Did you ever know any officer named Hoke?

Answer. Yes, sir, there were three; Major R. F. Hoke, afterwards major general, was from my regiment.

Question. Give the names of some of the officers connected with the regiment.

Answer. Colonel R. V. Cowan, Hutersville, North Carolina, 33d regiment; Colonel Joseph H. Saunders, North Carolina, (always in prison,) 33d regiment, from Rapidan station; Captain W. H. Lucus, of Baltimore—is engaged there in mercantile business; Captain G. W. Sanderlin, Pasquotank county; Captain J. A. Weston, Baltimore, law student.

Question. Do you know any others residing in Raleigh belonging to the regiment?

Answer. No, sir, I believe I am the only man.

Question. How long had Major Hoke been transferred when you joined it?

Answer. I do not know; he left the regiment at Orange Court House before I joined it, as lieutenant colonel. I resigned my lieutenancy on General Martin's staff to accept a second lieutenancy in 1864, in company H, of the 33d regiment.

Question. Did you know of any "local defence" organization here in 1864?

Answer. No, sir; I knew of the militia.

Question. Did you know General R. F. Hoke's brigade?

Answer. No, sir; if I could recollect the regiments of his brigade, I am sure I should know some of them; nor do I know where they were stationed. Lieutenant Justice, of my regiment, went on his staff; I do not know him, only by reputation; do not know where he resides.

Question. How was he transferred?

Answer. I think he went to General Hoke as adjutant of the regiment of which General Hoke was colonel, before the general's promotion.

Question. Did you ever hear of certain local defence organizations which were put in the confederate service?

Answer. I know of some bridge-guard companies, and also some partisan rangers, which were attached to our command.

Question. What were they?

Answer. Nethercutt's battalion; they were attached to us in 1863.

Question. Did you ever see any of them afterwards?

Answer. Yes, again at Petersburg, Virginia. They were formed into a regiment under General Martin in North Carolina.

Question. Were you ever associated with any of the members of Hoke's brigade directly or indirectly?

Answer. No, sir, not that I can recollect.

Ex. Doc. 98——5

Question. Were you ever at Newbern in 1864?
Answer. No, sir, not in the town; I was in Virginia from February, 1864.
Question. Are you positive you were never in Kinston after November, 1863?
Answer. No, sir; but I was not there after December 1.
Question. How many months were you there?
Answer. I think I arrived there about the 10th of August, 1863, and left about October or November, for Wilmington. I remained in Wilmington, taking out the two months I was away.
Question. Did you ever return to Kinston after going to Wilmington?
Answer. No, sir, I did not.
Question. In what capacity did you act while in Kinston, during the three months mentioned?
Answer. I was principally in the office of General Martin, first as acting aide-de-camp and in charge of the couriers.
Question. What brigade relieved you at Kinston?
Answer. I think Colquitt's brigade of Georgians.
Question. Do you know who relieved them?
Answer. No, sir; possibly Hoke's, but I am not sure.
Question. Do you recollect of any arrests being made?
Answer. No, sir, nothing but incidental police regulations.
Question. Do you recollect of the organization of troops into companies and regiments during that time?
Answer. I do.
Question. What organizations do you recollect of?
Answer. I recollect of the formation of the 66th regiment.
Question. In what month was it formed?
Answer. About September or October, 1863.
Question. Do you recollect under whose orders they were formed?
Answer. The war department at Richmond.
Question. From what source was this order promulgated, so far as your department was concerned?
Answer. I am not certain, but think it likely that General Martin should have issued an order.
Question. Did you have any conversation with the officers of that regiment in reference to its formation?
Answer. Yes, sir; Captain Sykes, who is dead.
Question. What was said?
Answer. I remember a contention as to who should be captain. Sykes was second lieutenant, and took the old captain's place; also that Nethercutt should be lieutenant colonel.
Question. Did you ever hear of any fluttering on the part of the privates?
Answer. Yes, sir; they volunteered for duty there in "Nethercutt's battalion," and did not want to leave home. After the 66th was formed, there was no fluttering at all.
Question. Was it not understood that those men termed volunteers were men who had volunteered into other organizations, and not into the 66th?
Answer. Yes, sir.
Question. Do you know of any desertions or escapes having been effected during the time they were in camp?
Answer. No, sir; but in bringing them up to general rendezvous many did not come and got away.
Question. Do you not remember that some other organization was used to collect these men?
Answer. No, sir; but Major Nethercutt advised that himself and some other influential officers should go down and persuade the men to come up. These

men could go to their homes almost every night, and did not like to go away, where it was unknown to them.

Question. In bringing the battalion up, how many came?

Answer. Not half of them.

Question. What brigade was the 66th assigned to after formation?

Answer. Martin's brigade, and went to Wilmington, and thence to Virginia.

Question. Do you know the names of any of General Martin's staff?

Answer. Yes, sir; Major A. Gordon, quartermaster, Ashville, North Carolina; Captain C. G. Elliot, assistant adjutant general, Pasquotank county.

Question. What regiments were in Martin's brigade at this time?

Answer. 42d, 50th, 17th, on detailed service. General Martin resides at Ashville, North Carolina.

Question. Did you ever see any of the 66th under guard?

Answer. Yes, sir; but do not remember what regiments.

Question. Was it not generally understood in the staff that it required a considerable force to keep this regiment together?

Answer. Yes, sir; Nethercutt had some men he could trust, who did guard duty, and who would have died for him.

Question. Did you ever hear of the 66th regiment being in any battle?

Answer. Oh, yes, sir, and they fought like men at Coal Harbor. A good many of the 66th afterwards joined the regiment; seeing the error of their ways, they would come in by squads, as the regiment was a long while in the State.

Question. Were there any orders or notices directing the arrest of such men as deserters who had not reported to the 66th?

Answer. Not that I remember.

Question. Did you ever hear of the execution of any alleged deserters from the 66th North Carolina?

Answer. No, sir; never heard of any, or know of any.

FEBRUARY 8, 1866.

Court of inquiry met, as per adjournment, from time to time during the absence of Lieutenant Wilcox and the clerk; after hearing the report of Lieutenant Wilcox, the recorder was instructed to summon John C. Tay, Major Hughes and Colonel Whitford, all of Newbern and vicinity.

Court then adjourned to meet at 10 o'clock a. m., February 9, 1866.

FEBRUARY 9, 1866.

Court met in pursuance to adjournment, all the members being present.

Samuel McDonald Tate, fourth witness, being duly sworn, deposes as follows:

My name is Samuel McDonald Tate; my age is thirty-five; my occupation is that of a gentleman.

Question. What was your occupation in the early part of the year 1864?

Answer. I was an officer in the confederate army, with the rank of lieutenant colonel.

Question. Were you in command of a regiment at that time?

Answer. Yes, the 6th North Carolina State troops, organized in 1862 for the war, and known as the regular army of the State of North Carolina.

Question. What brigade were you attached to in February and March, 1864?

Answer. Hoke's brigade—General R. F. Hoke.

Question. Where were you stationed at that time?

Answer. I think in the latter part of January, 1864, we were encamped on the Rapidan, Virginia, and ordered then to North Carolina, and came by way of Richmond and Petersburg to Kinston, where we remained until about the middle of April. We left Kinston and went to Plymouth, which I think we captured about the 20th of April.

Question. Who were the commanding officers of regiments while you were at Kinston?

Answer. General Lewis, then lieutenant colonel, commanded 43d North Carolina regiment a portion of the time, then the 21st Georgia regiment, commanded by a colonel who was afterwards killed at Plymouth, I forget his name; Lieutenant Colonel Hooper was lieutenant colonel of that regiment. There were four regiments and a battalion in the brigade, (the brigade proper.) The 43d North Carolina and 21st Georgia were detached from Lee's army and added to the brigade. The 6th regiment was commanded by myself; the 21st North Carolina regiment was commanded by Major Wm. J. Phofe; the 54th North Carolina regiment was commanded by Major Rogers; the 57th North Carolina regiment was commanded by Major James A. Craig; the 1st North Carolina battalion of sharpshooters, commanded by Captain Cooper, and a portion of this time by Captain Wilson, who had been severely wounded, so the command devolved upon Captain Cooper, who, on Captain Winslow's return, acted temporarily on General Hoke's staff. When orders were received for moving of troops from Virginia to the army of North Carolina, General Hoke communicated the information to me, and left the command in Virginia, turning it over to me. I brought the command through and overtook General Hoke at Petersburg, and again at Garysburg, North Carolina, and assumed command of the forces. I think he was in command from the time we met him in Garysburg, because there the detailed regiments joined, and the colonel of the Georgia regiment ranked me. This officer had been drinking, and General Hoke did not wish him to remain in command, so that I really commanded the brigade proper through what may be called the Newbern campaign. There were other brigades in the campaign.

Question. While at Kinston were there any other brigades stationed there?

Answer. Yes, sir; Kemper's Virginia brigade. Kemper was then a prisoner, and did not command.

Question. While at Kinston do you recollect of the execution of any deserters?

Answer. Yes, sir; about seventy-odd.

Question. Was Hoke's brigade present?

Answer. Yes, sir.

Question. Who was the commanding officer of all the forces in Kinston?

Answer. That is exceedingly hard to say.

Question. Did you see General Hoke in command at the execution?

Answer. Yes, sir; I took my regiment out to see the execution. I do not know who I got my orders from, Hoke or Corse; Corse was senior to Hoke, but was not always there. The order to take out my troops to the execution I think came from General Hoke, my brigade commander. I know a court-martial was convened there.

Question. What other regiments were present at the time of the execution?

Answer. Hoke's brigade was ordered to be present.

Question. How many executions did you attend?

Answer. Well, it was a sort of general hanging down there. There were so many executions that I was considerably worried at having to take my men over so often as there was such deep sand. At one time I think a dozen were hung.

Question. Do you know what these men were charged with?

Answer. After these men were carried out on to the field, before being executed, the proceedings of the court-martial's order convening court, &c., were read, as is usual.

Question. Do you know by whose order the execution took place?

Answer. Yes, sir; by order of General Pickett, commanding department. I know I saw General Hoke present at one of these hangings, and I think at the first one of these twelve.

Question. Was any detail made from your regiment to hang these twelve?

Answer. Not that I know of; I do not think I was called on for any detail for that specific purpose. The charges on which they were hung were desertion to the enemy, and seemed in each case to be pretty generally the same, and the specifications were to some of them that they were duly enlisted men in Nethercutt's and Whitford's battalions, and were in the "State" or "local" service.

Question. Were they not charged with being in arms against the Confederate States?

Answer. Some of them were, but not all. I think some of them were found at Batchelor's Creek, with United States uniforms on; I am sure one or more of those men had on blue pants and dark-blue blouse, and cap answering to the uniform of the United States.

Question. Will you state the *modus operandi* by which these twelve men were executed?

Answer. I think there was a square around the scaffold at a point about equidistance, and officers read the charges and specifications against the prisoners, and finding of court-martial, and the order for their execution. After this, some of the chaplains of the command made a public prayer in their behalf. The prisoners were then marched upon the scaffold, the ropes were adjusted around their necks, and, I believe, given in every instance an opportunity to make any remarks they wished to make. The trap was sprung under them and they were hung. We always waited until they were pronounced dead by the surgeons. I received orders to march off from General Hoke's staff officers.

Question. Did any of them make remarks?

Answer. I do not know if they did; I was too far removed to hear.

Question. In what month did this occur?

Answer. In February or March, while we were at Kinston.

Question. Did you ever have any conversation with General Hoke or any of his staff, in reference to these executions?

Answer. General Hoke and I were very intimate aside from official business; we were very social and friendly; had been raised in the same part of North Carolina. We have had so many conversations about the war, that it is quite likely. The occasion was one which would naturally cause it, but I cannot remember anything particularly. I do not recollect any particular conversation in reference to the men.

Question. Did you never make inquiries or desire any information except from hearing charges read?

Answer. Yes, sir, I presume I did. I heard several officers discuss the matter both before and after the hanging. It was understood that some of them ran into the United States lines to escape arrest.

Question. Do you know or have you any information of the commands to which the officers of the court-martial belonged, by whom these men were tried?

Answer. I have not the most remote idea. I do not think I ever heard, because I did not know really that there were such prisoners being tried until the proceedings were read out. They must have been tried by some division court-martial then in session, and not organized for that specific purpose. I was detailed on a court-martial, but do not think they were tried by that court. I got excused from serving, because we had but few officers in my regiment, and a large number of recruits, and I wanted to attend to them myself. The court was ordered by General Pickett, and I think convened after the execution of these men. My impression is that these men were executed in presence of Hoke's brigade, as an example to such as might be weak-kneed among the North Carolina soldiers.

Question. Do you recollect any of the chaplains attending these men?

Answer. Yes, sir; Chaplain John Varis, of the 54th North Carolina.

Question. What denomination?

Answer. Methodist, I think Protestant Methodist, from Virginia.

Question. Did you have any transferred men in your regiment from the local organizations of the State?

Answer. Yes, sir; from the reserves, but not from Whitford's or Nethercutt's battalions.

Question. Who composed General Hoke's staff?

Answer. Major Lyons was his commissary; Captain Adams, adjutant general's department; Lieutenant Justice, personal staff.

Question. Do you know where any of them reside?

Answer. I do not.

Question. Do you know where any of General G. E. Pickett's staff reside?

Answer. No, sir.

Question. Do you recollect who approved of the sentence against these men?

Answer. General G. E. Pickett. No one short of a commander of a department or army in the field could approve a death sentence.

Question. Do you know whether the men had any counsel allowed them?

Answer. No, sir; I know nothing about it more.

Question. How many of these executions did you attend?

Answer. Three or more. They began and increased until they got to be frightful. I think there were twenty-odd hung at the first time, but I am not positive to more than twelve, as I wish to be particular. In our service we shot a man for desertion; but for desertion to the enemy, which was a higher offence, we hung them, and that is why I think these men were hung.

Court adjourned until Saturday, February 10, 1866, 10 o'clock a. m.

FEBRUARY 10, 1866—10 o'clock a. m.

Court convened in pursuance to adjournment, all the members being present. The minutes of the last meeting were read and approved.

Fifth witness, Mr. Englehart, clerk of the senate of North Carolina, appeared, was sworn, and stated that he was a major in the adjutant general's department of the confederate army, under General Lee, and knew nothing about the army of North Carolina in the year 1864, only as he read accounts of it in the papers, being stationed at the time on the Rapidan river, in Virginia.

Sixth witness, Oscar Eastmond, sworn:

My name is Oscar Eastmond; am 26 years of age; am a liquor dealer byoccupation, and reside in Raleigh, North Carolina. In the early part of 1864, I was captain of the 1st North Carolina volunteers, (loyal.) I was stationed at Little Washington in the months of February and March, 1864. I afterwards became commander of the regiment. I knew a man by the name of Swayne, who was tried by the same court that condemned the men hung at Kinston. in the early part of 1864. He now resides at or near Washington, North Carolina.

Seventh witness, Caleb Gaylod, sworn:

My name is Caleb Gaylod; I reside in Raleigh, North Carolina; I am 18 years of age; I was a soldier in the early part of 1864, in 1st North Carolina cavalry, (loyal Union;) I was not present at the execution of Union prisoners at Kinston, North Carolina, in 1864, but heard of it; I do not know of any person on the trial of these men.

ROOMS COURT OF INQUIRY,
February 15, 1866.

Court met in pursuance of adjournment, all being present except the president, absent by orders from headquarters department of North Carolina.

Eighth witness, John Hughes, sworn, who testified as follows: Reside in

Newbern, North Carolina; my occupation a lawyer; am thirty-five years of age; I was in the confederate army in 1864.

Question. In what capacity were you acting?

Answer. I was quartermaster in Hoke's brigade.

Question. Where were you stationed in February and March, 1864?

Answer. At Kinston, North Carolina. His adjutant, James Adams; John A. Cooper, aide-de-camp; John G. Justice, aide-de-camp; Major J. W. Lyon, commissary; Sed. Guion, ordnance officer; Dr. Vernon, brigade surgeon. Adams resides in Lewisburg, North Carolina; Cooper resides in Iredell county, North Carolina; Justice resides in Lincolnton county, North Carolina; Lyon resides in Baltimore, Maryland; Guion resides in Mecklenburg county, North Carolina; Dr. Vernon resides at Shepherdstown, Virginia. I remember of the execution of alleged deserters at Kinston, North Carolina; in the early part of 1864. I remember of some twenty-odd being hung for desertion to the enemy. At the time of the battle of Batchelor's creek, North Carolina, these men were captured. I was in Virginia; had been left at Gordonsville by General Hoke, in charge of baggage and transportation during the temporary absence of the brigade in North Carolina. I was ordered to Kinston, and reached there upon the day, I think, of the execution of thirteen of these deserters, ten, I think, having been previously executed. I therefore cannot of my personal knowledge state that there was a court-martial, but I was informed, at the time of the execution of the thirteen men above mentioned, that the whole number had been duly tried and condemned to be hung by a regularly constituted court-martial. I witnessed the execution, which was conducted in the usual form, in the presence of all the troops then in the vicinity of Kinston; the condemned being attended and ministered to at the time of their execution by the brigade chaplain. The reason why I made the inquiry was, I was a lawyer and felt interested in the matter; it was the only execution by hanging I had ever witnessed in the army. My impression is, I spoke with General Hoke on the subject; I was on terms of intimacy with the general, and messed with him. I asked the general when these men had been tried and who constituted the court; I think he stated that they had been tried soon after they were brought to Kinston, and that he gave me a statement of the members of the court; I cannot recollect one of them at present. He stated that they had been tried in two separate parties. I think the court was composed of Virginians; no North Carolinians and Georgians. I was so far from the scaffold I could not hear the charges read. I think they all had federal uniforms on. I was informed that they had deserted from Whitford's and Nethercutt's commands. I was informed that the order was from General G. E. Pickett ordering their execution, who commanded the department at the time. I saw them buried under the scaffold. I saw the body of a man executed removed by his wife. I saw the graves dug and the place where they were buried afterwards. The troops were transferred by the State to the confederate government without re-enlisting.

Ninth witness, John N. Whitford, sworn: My name is John N. Whitford; reside in Jones county; my home is in Newbern; I am thirty-one years of age; my occupation is a farmer. In 1864 I was in the service of the State of North Carolina; I was a lieutenant colonel of a battalion in the early part of 1864, called Whitford's battalion, afterwards the 67th North Carolina State troops for "local defence." The terms of enlistment were, not to be removed out of the State of North Carolina. They enlisted as State troops. The way in which the 67th was formed was in the formation of new companies to be attached to Whitford's battalion.

I was not present at Kinston at the time of the execution of the alleged deserters; I was on picket duty. Some of my command were even arrested as deserters. Rufus W. Horton was inspector general of Hoke's brigade; he resides at Washington.

The court adjourned until February 16, 1866, at ten o'clock a. m.

FEBRUARY 16, 1866—10 o'clock a. m.

In consequence of the absence of the president of the court, per special order No. 40, ex. 4, dated headquarters department of North Carolina, February 13th, 1866, directing the president to proceed to New York on public business, the court adjourned until February 23, 1866, at 10 oclock a. m.

FEBRUARY 23, 1866—10 o'clock a. m.

Court met in pursuance of adjournment, all the members being present, and adjourned to the 1st of March, 1866, to await the attendance of witnesses.

MARCH 1, 1866—10 o'clock a. m.

Court met in pursuance of adjournment, all the members being present. The witnesses summoned not being in attendance, the court adjourned to the 2d March, 1866, at 10 o'clock a. m.

MARCH 2, 1866—10 o'clock a. m.

Court met in pursuance of adjournment, all the members being present.

Tenth witness, Z. B. Vance, being duly sworn, deposed as follows:

My name is Z. B. Vance; reside in Statesville, North Carolina; was governor of North Carolina in 1864, and resided in Raleigh.

Question. State what you know about the status of the State troops or organizations for local defence of the State of North Carolina in 1863 and 1864.

Answer. There were two classes, home guards or militia, and State troops which could not leave the State without my authority. General Martin, of eastern North Carolina, ordered these detached bodies into the 66th regiment. Nethercutt's battalion rebelled against it, and went in not very cheerfully. The great difficulty did not arise until the regiment was ordered to Wilmington, claiming that they were raised for local defence around the Neuse river, &c. Some 250 or 300 took to the woods and refused to go, but all came up except about fifty.

No official report was made to me of the execution of the deserters at Kinston in federal uniforms. Major General Pickett, I believe, was in command of the expedition, and being superior to General Martin, temporarily took command. I think General Tony Baker was in command instead of General Martin.

There was some account in the newspapers of the hanging of twenty.

I am inclined to think the confederate government did not keep faith with those local troops, who were found to be of little, if any, benefit to the service.

I know Colonel Fenabee, who raised a command for the local service on the Chowan river, was forced into the regular service by the confederate government.

I did at various times make appeals to confederate authorities in behalf of men of this State. These men were enlisted entirely for local defence, and every effort was made to transfer these organizations into the regular service of the confederacy when they were found to be worthless.

I myself favored transfer to regular service where it could be done without violation of good faith, but though in these instances of Nethercutt's battalion it was a violation of their enlistment agreements.

My impression is that the first I heard was of the execution of these men.

Court then adjourned until March 6, 1866, at 10 o'clock a. m.

MARCH 6, 1866—10 o'clock a. m.

Court met pursuant to adjournment, and, for absence of witnesses, adjourned to meet March 7, 1866, at 10 o'clock a. m.

MARCH 7, 1866—10 o'clock a. m.

Court met in pursuance of adjournment, absent Lieutenant Penniman, recorder

Eleventh witness, John G. Justice, sworn: Am twenty-one years of age; reside in Lincolnton, North Carolina. In fore part of 1864 was lieutenant and aide-de-camp on the staff of Brigadier General R. F. Hoke. In the months of January, February, March, and first few days of April, was stationed at Kinston. I knew of the execution of certain alleged deserters from the confederate army at Kinston in those months, who had been captured from the Union forces, and was present at the execution. I remember the name of but one of the captured, called Jackson.

Question. Who were on the court-martial that tried these men?

Answer. I do not recollect.

Question. State what regiment they had belonged to in the rebel army?

Answer. The first two hung belonged to company B, 10th North Carolina artillery; the others I do not know.

Queston. How many executions were there of these men taken from the Union lines?

Answer. I think there were twenty-one, possibly more.

Question. How many executions did you attend?

Answer. I was present at only two executions. In the first, two were hung; in the next, five were hung.

Question. Who was in command at that time, and who issued the orders for the execution of these men?

Answer. Major General G. E. Pickett commanded the department of East North Carolina at that time. I cannot say positively who issued orders for the execution of these men, but I presume General Pickett ordered it, as he, being commandant, was the only person who possibly had authority so to do in the department of East North Carolina.

Question. What did your brigade or its commander do in the matter of the execution of these alleged deserters?

Answer. Our troops were present under command of Colonel Mercer—I mean General Hoke's brigade—at those which I was present; I think they were present at the other executions, but did not see them there.

Question. Where was General R. F. Hoke at these executions?

Answer. I can't possibly say; about that time he was getting up an expedition. I think he was present at the first execution, in command of his brigade; Colonel Mercer commanded at the others and not at the first.

Question. Who ordered your brigade out on these occasions?

Answer. I could not say, but think it was optional with the general to take his brigade there. I do not think he had any orders, but presume he asked permission of General Pickett to take his brigade out; at the first execution company B, 10th North Carolina artillery, was present, to which the two men hung belonged.

Question. What other troops were present at those executions?

Answer. No other troops were present at those executions, except at one time Colonel Whitford's regiment; other troops came there, but merely as spectators, and not as organized troops.

Question. If General Hoke had not asked permission to take his brigade out, would orders have been given for the presence of troops?

Answer. Yes, sir; troops would have been ordered out, as they are always present at executions.

Question. Who hung these men?

Answer. There was an officer and guard detailed to superintend the hanging.

Question. How many of the men hung were tried by court-martial?

Answer. I do not know, sir, as to any.

Question. Where or to what authority did the proceedings of court-martials in the case of any of these men go to, provided they were tried by court-martial?

Answer. The proceedings were, of course, forwarded to the commandant ordering the court. In our brigade we had a "special order" book in which court-martial proceedings were copied of men tried from our brigade; I tried to look it up the day I received my summons to appear here, but could not find it; the book was lost at the surrender.

Question. How many of these men executed were from Hoke's brigade?

Answer. I don't think any were.

Question. What regiments were then in Hoke's brigade?

Answer. 6th North Carolina, 57th North Carolina, 54th North Carolina, 21st North Carolina, and 21st Georgia, and 43d North Carolina temporarily attached.

Question. To what brigade or under whose immediate command was Nethercutt's battalion, or the 66th North Carolina regiment?

Answer. At that time it was formed into the 66th cavalry, A. D. More's regiment, and I presume was under General Martin at Wilmington; as it was not attached to our command, I cannot say positively where it was, but think it was at Wilmington; there shortly afterwards, as we sent some deserters down there to it.

Question. State whom General Palmer, commanding Union forces at Newbern, corresponded with in your army in reference to the hanging of these men.

Answer. General Palmer corresponded with General Pickett; the correspondence was published in the papers of the State. General Hoke is very anxious that this matter of hanging these men should be investigated, which was the reason of my trying to find the book, because, although these men did not belong to our brigade, as we were at the execution it is presumed their sentences were copied in our special order book.

Question. Who read the sentence at these executions, where your brigade attended?

Answer. I read them once when the five men were hung; other staff officers of our brigade read at other occasions.

Question. Do you remember, except as to the 10th North Carolina artillery, to what regiments or commands any of these men belonged, or by whose orders those sentences were carried into effect?

Answer. No, sir; I presume the order for execution was from General Pickett. I don't think General Hoke could have issued these orders, as he was a subordinate officer.

Question. Do you know what was the character and enlistment agreements of the organizations composing the 66th North Carolina regiment?

Answer. No, sir, I do not; we were brigaded at that time, and knew but little of outside organizations. They were afterwards in our division, but never saw them until carried to Virginia.

Question. Where were you the day thirteen men were executed?

Answer. I staid in my quarters then.

Question. Did you ever talk with these men of the 66th as to the way they came into service?

Answer. No, sir, not directly; they were organized and did duty around their homes, where they were of no use, and when ordered to form the 66th, many of Nethercutt's battalion went to their homes between the lines. General Pickett, I think, issued a proclamation telling these men that they had done wrong, and if they came in and surrendered themselves they would be let off without punishment. Many did come in by squads and were furnished transportation to Wilmington to their regiments.

Question. Did those men who were hung desert before the organization of the 66th North Carolina, or afterwards?

Answer. I do not know.

Question. Who composed General Hoke's staff at that time?
Answer. James M. Adams, captain and assistant adjutant general, living now near Lincolnton, North Carolina; John Cooper, captain and assistant inspector general, Statesville, North Carolina; myself, as aide-de-camp; Thomas Grier, lieutenant and ordnance officer, Charlotte, North Carolina.

Twelfth witness, William Gaston Lewis, sworn: Aged 30; reside in Charlotte, North Carolina.
Question. What was your occupation in the early part of 1864?
Answer. Lieutenant colonel, commanding 43d North Carolina regiment.
Question. Where were you stationed in February and March?
Answer. At Kinston and below there. I left Kinston on thirty days' leave about March 11.
Question. State what you know of the execution in these months of certain alleged deserters from the rebel army who were captured from the Union forces.
Answer. I was absent when a portion were executed, and at the other times was on detached service, cleaning out obstructions from the Neuse river.
Question. Who were on the court-martial that tried these men?
Answer. I do not know.
Question. State what regiment they belonged to.
Answer. I do not know.
Question. Who was in command at Kinston then, and who issued orders for their execution?
Answer. General Pickett was in command at the expedition when they were captured. I was on detached service by order of General Hoke, in whose brigade I was. General Hoke, I think, reported to General Lee direct, but was under General Pickett's orders on that expedition. The thing seemed somewhat mixed.
Question. Who gave you leave of absence?
Answer. No one; General Hoke said he could not give me one as he would have to go to Brigadier General M. D. Corse, and General Corse did not seem inclined to grant such; on the contrary, General Hoke gave me an order to go to Tarborough on special duty, under which I went home. The day after I left an order came from General Corse to my quarters detailing me on a court-martial to try Colonel Baker.
Question. To whom did the court-martial proceedings have to go in capital cases involving death during that time at Kinston?
Answer. To the commander of the department, Major General Pickett.
Question. Would the hanging of those men at Kinston without his approval or order have been a violation of the rules of war?
Answer. We did not confine ourselves to regulations as strictly as in the United States service. Our commanders in departments or armies frequently changed the articles of war and regulations by their orders.
Question. What military authority in the so-called confederate armies had the power of executing the sentence of death awarded by courts-martial on any person?
Answer. I think only the commander of an army or department. These were frequently suspended by order of armies and departments, and it was matter of remark in our army that they were almost a dead letter.
Question. Do you remember of any correspondence between General Palmer at Newbern and Major General Pickett, in reference to the hanging of these men?
Answer. Yes, sir; General Hoke, when I got back, showed me a despatch from General Palmer, which he was forwarding, I think, to General Pickett, but am not positive, threatening retaliation if the men captured from his lines were hung.
Question. What was your last capacity in the rebel army?

Answer. Brigadier general in the regular confederate army.

Question. Do you remember anything further in reference to the hanging of these men ?

Answer. No, sir, I did not see any of them, by being absent on detached service just at that time; I had no opportunities of knowing, I do not know, who gave the order for executing those men, nor who were on the court-martial which tried them.

Question. On that campaign did you know or hear of the summary execution of any alleged deserters ?

Answer. No, sir; those that were executed were all tried by regular court-martial.

Court then adjourned until 10 o'clock a. m., on March 8, 1866.

Court met on Thursday, March 8, 1866, 10 o'clock a. m. All the members present except Lieutenant Penniman.

Minutes and evidence taken at previous meeting read. Owing to absence of witnesses who had been summoned, the board adjourned to 9th instant, at 10 o'clock a. m.

MARCH 9, 1866—10 o'clock a. m.

13th. John C. Washington appeared and was sworn.

Question. State your name, age and place of residence.

Answer. John C. Washington; age, sixty-four, and reside in the county of Lenoir, near town of Kinston.

Question. What was your occupation and where were you early in the year 1864, in January, February, March, April and May?

Answer. I was a planter and frequently at home in Kinston, though travelling considerably; I think I was at home the whole of that time.

Question. What was the reason of your travelling so frequently at that time?

Answer. Simply for amusement.

Question. State what you know of the capture from the Union forces at that time of certain alleged deserters from the rebel army.

Answer. I only know there were a number of persons brought to Kinston, and saw them there and understood they were captured near Newbern. I understood there were two classes of them; some were deserters from our army, who had joined the federal army, and some who had joined the federal army from below, between the lines, and were not deserters.

Question. Did you know any of these men ?

Answer. It is probable I did; one I knew and conversed with him, named Clinton Cox, from my county. If I heard their names I might recall them.

Question. State fully what you know of Clinton Cox's capture; what was done with him, and the substance of your conversation.

Answer. I went to see Clinton Cox, and had a talk with him; I feared he had previously joined our army and might be hung; I asked him how he came below at Newbern? He said he had been sent to Salisbury, escaped from there and went down the river and joined the federal army. Previous to that, he said he had not joined the rebel army. He did not state, to my recollection, why he had been sent to Salisbury, and I do not know whether he had been conscripted.

Question. Were any of those men captured members of Nethercutt's battalion; if so, state how many ?

Answer. I do not know; my impression is, some of them were; I knew Nethercutt, but his men were mostly from below.

Question. State whether Clinton Cox was tried by a court-martial and what was done with him.

Answer. He was said to have been tried by court-martial, at Kinston, and then sent to Richmond. I think I was away then.

Question. Who commanded at Kinston at that time?

Answer. My impression is that General Hoke was the commander there, but General G. E. Pickett commanded the department.

Question. State what you know of a court-martial being held there, for the trial of these captured men.

Answer. I only know it was reported that a court-martial was held there, but was never in the room.

Question. Who were on the court-martial that tried these men?

Answer. I do not know; possibly I heard, but have not the slightest recollection.

Question. How many executions were there of the captured men?

Answer. I understood twenty-two or twenty-three. I was not present at the execution. I was present on the field when two were to be executed, but when the rope was put around their necks turned my back and left.

Question. To whom did the findings of the court, sentencing these men, go for approval?

Answer. I understood they went to General Pickett.

Question. State any conversation ever held with any officers of the rebel army on duty there, in reference to this matter.

Answer. I have no recollection of any. General Pickett was once or twice at my house; General Hoke frequently, and other officers.

Question. Who issued orders for the execution of these men?

Answer. I have no recollection; I presume General Pickett did.

Question. Who had the right to award sentence of death on prisoners in the so-called confederate army?

Answer. I do not know, but presume the commanding officer of the post or department.

Question. State if any of these men were hung without trial by court-martial.

Answer. I don't know. In the case of this man Cox, he was found not guilty, as not having joined the rebel army.

Question. When you went on the field at the execution you attended, who commanded the troops present, and what troops were present?

Answer. My impression is General Hoke's brigade was present, under his command.

Question. Previous to putting the rope around the neck, at the execution you attended, state what proceedings were had there.

Answer. The troops were drawn out in hollow square, but I was not near enough to hear any sentence or court-martial proceedings read. I was distant one hundred or two hundred yards.

Question. State whether there was any conversation among the people of Kinston as to the justness of the hanging of these men, and the general opinion.

Answer. My impression is that there was, considerable, but being removed from much intercourse with them, I cannot recall what it was.

Question. State, if you know, what were the terms of enlistment of the "partisan rangers," or Nethercutt's battalion.

Answer. I know but little. I thought they were rather a free kind of troops.

Question. Who were the generals there at that time?

Answer. General Pickett, General R. F. Hoke, General Seth Barton, and General Corse.

Question. State whom you know of those executed.

Answer. Stephen Jones is the only one whose name I am familiar with.

George W. Quinn appeared, and was sworn as fourteenth witness.

Question. State your name, age, and place of residence.

Answer. George W. Quinn; twenty-seven years old, and live in Kinston, North Carolina.

Question. What was your occupation in the months of January, February, March, April, and May, 1864, and where stationed?

Answer. I was a soldier in the 67th North Carolina regiment, State troops, and stationed at Kinston.

Question. In what capacity were you acting?

Answer. I was acting as military courier at headquarters in Kinston.

Question. What headquarters?

Answer. Headquarters of the post commander, Brigadier General Seth Barton.

Question. Who commanded the department of Eastern North Carolina?

Answer. Major General G. E. Pickett.

Question. What other generals were there?

Answer. General Corse of Virginia, General R. F. Hoke of North Carolina, General Matt. Ransom of North Carolina, General Barton, and General J. G. Martin.

Question. State fully what you know in reference to the capture, from the Union lines, and execution of certain alleged deserters at Kinston in this period.

Answer. I knew some of those men who were captured down near Newbern from the federal army—Jesse Summer, the two Freemans, and another whose name I cannot recall, but whom I knew before the war.

Question. To what regiments had these men belonged?

Answer. Most of them, I think, were from Nethercutt's battalion.

Question. What kind of an organization was that?

Answer. They were raised as "local State troops," for the defence of Eastern North Carolina, and when turned over to be organized into a regiment, with bridge guard companies, and called the 66th North Carolina, many of the men deserted at the time they were ordered away, and a portion joined the federal army.

Question. Where do you mean they were ordered to?

Answer. From Kinston to Wilmington, where they were ordered to, for the purpose of being put into this regiment. They mistrusted what was going to happen, and so cleared out—some for their homes, and some for the federal lines.

Question. When were they ordered to Wilmington?

Answer. About November, 1863. I was in Kinston at the time.

Question. Where was their regiment, the 66th, when these men were executed?

Answer. It was, I think, at Wilmington, and not at Kinston.

Question. Were these men tried by court-martial?

Answer. It was said they were, but I was never present.

Question. Who composed the court?

Answer. I think by officers of General Pickett's division, principally Virginians. I do not know any of their names; I think it is likely that General Hoke was a member.

Question. State if you were present at any executions.

Answer. No, sir; never to any.

Question. How many were executed.

Answer. Two the first time; five the second; and thirteen, I think, the third time.

Question. Who issued the order for the executions?

Answer. I do not know.

Question. State if any of these men were executed without trial.

Answer. I think the first two hung were executed without trial. They were hung the day after we got back from the Newbern expedition. It took us one day to come up. I think they were of the 10th North Carolina artillery originally.

Question. Who were present at the executions?

Answer. I don't know, but I think General Barton issued an order for all the troops present to go. I did not. I never saw the prisoners to have any conversation with them.

Question. What was the general opinion among the people at Kinston?

Answer. That these men ought not to have been hung. They belonged to "Nethercutt's battalion," and enlisted, so it was believed, on a distinct promise, as several of the men of that battalion told me, that they were never to be sent above the Wilmington and Weldon railroad, and that their commander, Major Nethercutt, made this promise; many of the battalion did not think it was desertion to leave it and join the federal army when ordered into the 66th; the battalion was called, previous to consolidation, the 8th North Carolina battalion. I tried several times to go into the prison to see those I knew, but the guard would not let me, having orders to that effect.

Question. Recall, if possible, the names of these men.

Answer. I knew John Freeman, who was hung, also Jesse J. Summerlin, whom I knew very well; Andrew J. Britton, of Nethercutt's battalion, as also Stephen Jones, same troops; Elijah Kellum and Lewis Freeman, same troops. I know nothing further of the hanging and sentencing of these men.

The court adjourned to meet at headquarters department of North Carolina, on March 9, 1866, at 10 o'clock a. m.

MARCH 9, 1866—10 o'clock a. m.

Court met pursuant to adjournment.

Present: First Lieutenant and Adjutant A. B. Gardner, Second Lieutenant William K. Wilcox, 28th Michigan volunteers; absent, Lieutenant Penniman.

Minutes and testimony of previous meeting read and approved.

Owing to absence of witnesses who had been summoned, court adjourned until March 10, 1866, at 10 o'clock a. m.

MARCH 10, 1866—10 o'clock a. m.

Court met pursuant to adjournment, all the members being present; no witnesses being present, the court adjourned until the 16th instant, at 10 o'clock a. m.

MARCH 16, 1866—10 o'clock a. m.

Court met in pursuance of adjournment, all the members being present; no witnesses being in attendance, the court adjourned until March 17, 1866, at 10 o'clock a. m.

Court met on Saturday, March 17, 1866, at 10 o'clock a. m.

15th witness, Blunt King, appeared, and being duly sworn, testified as follows:

Question. State your name, age, and place of residence and present occupation.

Answer. Blunt King; forty-eight years of age; reside in Goldsborough, North Carolina, and am assistant chief of police.

Question. What was your occupation and where did you reside in the months of February, March, and April, 1864?

Answer. I was in Goldsborough, and was a private in the 10th North Carolina infantry, company B.

Question. State whether you were in Kinston during those months.

Answer. I think I was, in March, 1864, at Kinston for one day only.

Question. What was the occasion of your being there?

Answer. I went down on the first Newbern raid and stopped there coming back. Our company was with a pontoon train, and was delayed there a day waiting for transportation for the pontoons on the railroad.

Question. Did you have on soldier clothes then?

Answer. Only partially; I often had citizen's clothes on.

Question. What was your captain's name?

Answer. Captain Daniel Coggwell, of Raleigh.

Question. Do you recollect of seeing any prisoners hung there at Kinston?

Answer. Yes, sir.

Question. How did you come to be at the place of hanging?

Answer. Captain Adams, the adjutant general of Hoke's staff, ordered me there. The orders were to go up to the gallows with some ropes; and two other men, whom I don't remember, received similar orders.

Question. When you went to the gallows with these ropes, what did you do?

Answer. I handed them to a man, who put them over a beam and tied them; I was sitting playing cards on the pontoon boats at the depot; we were waiting for transportation; Captain Adams, of General Hoke's staff, came down to the depot and got some ropes from the pontoon boats, picking them out, I think, himself, and then said to us, "Who can tie a good hangman's knot;" some of the boys with whom I was playing said I was good at tying a knot; I said if General Pickett wanted any hanging done he had better do it himself. "What's that you say," said Captain Adams; I saw I was getting into trouble, and said, "I could beat any man playing seven up;" Captain Adams then said he would send for me in a few minutes, and did so. The reason I know it was Captain Adams, of General Hoke's staff, was because I inquired.

Question. What were the names of those two men you assisted in hanging?

Answer. Joseph Haskell and David Jones.

Question. How do you come to know their names?

Answer. They were in the company I belonged to.

Question. What were they hung for?

Answer. Desertion, I think.

Question. Were they captured from the Union forces? If so, state where.

Answer. They were captured somewhere near Batchelor's creek, but I was not with the party which captured them.

Question. State how you knew they had previously been members of your company.

Answer. Because they had both fought in Fort Macon, I believe, not being then a member myself; but when I joined the company they were members of it, wearing the rebel uniform, and in our company long before they deserted.

Question. State what was done at the execution of these men.

Answer. I was standing in the end of the wagon with the old minister; Captain Adams was standing off about ten feet from the gallows; there were three or four other men, private soldiers, present; I think I adjusted the rope about the neck of one, but of which I cannot remember. I think Captain Adams read some orders before they were hung; but what the orders were I don't remember; these men were executed the third day after they were caught.

Question. Where were you when you first saw these two men who were hung?

Answer. We were falling back; I first saw them in Dover about sunset, and should not have known them had not my lieutenant, Lieutenant H. M. Whitehead, who resides near Newbern, called my attention to them. I said, "Good evening, boys;" they said "Good evening, Mr. King." That was all I said, and sat down on a log near the fire, where they were standing; it was right at General Pickett's headquarters in Dover, North Carolina. I had gone up with two or three other soldiers to see them, out of curiosity. Before I sat down General G. E. Pickett come out of his tent, which was a large wall tent, and came up within four or five feet of these prisoners, and took Lieutenant Whitehead a little to one side and asked him about these two men. I heard Lieutenant Whitehead say they belonged to his company. General Pickett then walked up to the prisoners and said, "What are you doing here; where have you been?" They answered something which I did not hear; General Pickett then said, "God damn you, I reckon you will hardly ever go back there again, you damned rascals; I'll have you shot, and all other damned rascals who desert." Jones then said to Pickett "He did not care a damn whether they shot him then, or what they did with him." General Pickett then ordered him to be taken away from his tent. General Corse and General Hoke were standing by when General Pickett said this.

Question. Did you recognize any other of the prisoners there?
Answer. No, sir; I do not think I knew any others of them.
Question. What kind of uniforms did these prisoners have on?
Answer. I think they were dressed in blue; but don't remember either at that time or when Jones and Haskell were hung.
Question. State if these men said they belonged to the United States forces.
Answer. No, sir; not to my knowledge.
Question. Who commanded the rebel army there at this time when these two men were captured and hung?
Answer. Major General Pickett did.
Question. State whether you recollect one of the men assisting at the execution as having a squint or cross-eyes.
Answer. No, sir.
Question. What officers did you see at the execution of these two men?
Answer. General Hoke was close by with his brigade. I heard some of the boys say that General Pickett was there as we marched off after the execution, but I did not see him.
Question. Were you present at the execution of any of these others?
Answer. No, sir.
Question. State whether you volunteered your services at this execution or was ordered.
Answer. I did not volunteer; I was ordered by Captain Adams, the adjutant general of Hoke. I was vexed at being ordered on this duty, as I was playing cards at the time, and so made sure to find out Captain Adams's name.
Question. State whether you ever served in the army previous to entering the 10th North Carolina rebel infantry.
Answer. I was sergeant in company B, 1st North Carolina volunteers, and was in Mexico two years during our war there.
Question. State if you know whether these two men or any of those captured were tried by court-martial.
Answer. I do not know; I never knew any members of any such court.
Question. How do you come to think there was any such court?
Answer. When I was sitting on the log at Dover, after the prisoners had been taken away, General Pickett said: "We'll have to have a court-martial on these fellows pretty soon, and after some are shot the rest will stop deserting," or some similar expression. Then old General Corse answered, "The sooner the better." My lieutenant, Whitehead, then nudged me with his elbow and said, "You hear what they are saying?" A moment after we got up and went away. I heard General Pickett say, when within four miles from Newbern when we went down on this march, "That every God-damned man who didn't do his duty, or deserted, ought to be shot or hung." He was saying this to some soldier, but whether of our brigade or not I don't know. The paper I hand you was written for me, and in my presence, by H. M. Whitehead, who was the lieutenant of my company in the 10th North Carolina, whom I have been speaking about.

The court adjourned to the 21st of March, at 10 a. m., for the purpose of procuring in the mean time further testimony.

COURT OF INQUIRY, *Wednesday, March* 21, 1866—10 o'clock a. m.

Sixteenth witness, Drury Lacy, was sworn.

Question. State your name, age, place of residence and present occupation.

Answer. Drury Lacy; twenty-six years of age; reside in Raleigh, North Carolina, and am in the Southern Express Company.

Question. What was your occupation in the months of February, March, and April, 1864?

Answer. I was adjutant of the 43d North Carolina regiment, in R. F. Hoke's brigade, and in April was transferred to the same brigade staff as adjutant general to General Lewis, promoted.

Question. Where were you stationed?

Answer. In the neighborhood of Kinston, North Carolina, at that time.

Question. State to what brigade you were attached, and who commanded all the forces there at that time?

Answer. I was attached to General R. F. Hoke's brigade, and Major General G. E. Pickett commanded the department. Brigadier General Corse, under him, commanded the district in which Kinston was.

Question. State what you remember of the capture from the Union forces of certain alleged deserters from the rebel army, and their execution at that time.

Answer. I know there were about twenty or more captured and hung at different times at Kinston, though captured at the same time near Batchelor's creek.

Question. What regiments did those men belong to in the rebel army from which they were said to have deserted?

Answer. I believe the 10th North Carolina artillery; others to a battalion known as "Nethercutt's battalion."

Question. State whether all these prisoners were tried by court-martial previous to the execution.

Answer. I believe they were.

Question. State who composed the court.

Answer. I do not know the names of any. There were two courts sitting at different times, composed principally of Virginians, as there were four Virginia brigades in General Pickett's division proper in the department, and only one North Carolina brigade there at Kinston. I know Lieutenant Colonel Lewis was detailed on one of these courts, but was away. Lieutenant Colonel Tate, of the 6th North Carolina, was detailed on one of these courts.

Question. State whether you were present at any of these executions; and if so, which ones?

Answer. I saw the first two hung, and thirteen at another time; I may have seen more, but of these I am certain.

Question. State who ordered these executions.

Answer. The sentences of the court were reviewed by Major General Pickett, and it was by his order that the execution took place. Captain Stewart Symington, aide-de-camp to General Pickett, was his acting assistant adjutant general, and the orders were signed, I think, by him; General Pickett's real headquarters were at Petersburg, Virginia, where his adjutant general remained, which was the reason of the order being signed by Captain Symington.

Question. Who ordered the courts-martial sitting at Kinston during these months of 1864?

Answer. I think the court by which these men were tried was ordered by General Pickett. The other courts, I believe, by the district commander, General Corse.

Question. State whether any of these captured Union soldiers were executed in these months at Kinston without trial?

Answer. Not that I know of. I am almost certain not.

Question. In case of any necessity for a capital punishment or execution during these months at Kinston, or in eastern North Carolina, who alone had the authority to order them?

Answer. General Pickett. No other general in that department at that time had authority to order any execution.

Question. State if any officer in the rebel army in North Carolina at that time had authority to order any capital punishment without full and fair trial before court-martial.

Answer. No, sir; no officer had.

Question. State whether these men, said to have belonged to Nethercutt's battalion, and executed then at Kinston, were regularly in the confederate army.

Answer. I think they were; though most of the troops organized in the eastern part of the State of North Carolina were organized not to go out of the State, but were under confederate officers, when present; this battalion was one of that class of troops.

Question. State whether these men were deserters from "Nethercutt's battalion" or after it was consolidated into the 66th North Carolina.

Answer. I do not know, but think they deserted *before* consolidation; when they were executed the consolidation had taken place.

Question. Who commanded the troops at the execution you witnessed there and what troops were present?

Answer. At the execution of the two of the 10th North Carolina, to which I think they belonged, all the troops who had been on the Newbern expedition were present, or at least a large majority. I think General Pickett was present. General Corse was senior to General R. F. Hoke, and would have commanded if General Pickett had not been present. The execution was under the immediate direction of General Hoke, his surgeon being in attendance, and staff officers reading the orders. At the execution of the thirteen, I don't remember any other troops present besides our own or Hoke's brigade. General Hoke was not present, being, I think, on other duties. The direction of the execution was in charge of the senior officer of the brigade present, and General Hoke's staff officers reading orders, &c.

Question. Who were these orders from?

Answer. From Major General G. E. Pickett. I think I saw five others hung at one time, but my impression is General Hoke was not present, except at the first. I am certain General Pickett ordered the first execution of the two men, and I believe in each of the others, though they might have been ordered by General Corse or General Hoke, but they would have had no right so to do, unless *pro tem.* in command of the department or acting immediately under General Pickett's orders.

Question. State why Hoke's brigade was always selected for attendance at these executions.

Answer. I don't know.

Question. State if you recollect any correspondence between General Palmer, of the United States forces at Newbern, and any officer of your army in reference to the hanging of these men.

Answer. Not that I remember. There was some discussion among the officers as to the number hung, though not to any extent.

Seventeenth witness, General Martin, sworn.

Question. State, if you please, your name, age, and place of residence.

Answer. James G. Martin, forty-four years of age, and reside in Asheville, North Carolina.

Question. What was your occupation during the months of February, March, and April, 1864, and where stationed?

Answer. I was a brigadier general in the Confederate States army, and was stationed in Wilmington in those months, and left there latter part of April.

Question. What troops were in your command there at that time?

Answer. The 17th North Carolina, 42d North Carolina, the 50th North Carolina, and the 66th North Carolina regiments.

Question. State, if you please, what the 66th North Carolina was, and how composed.

Answer. It was composed principally of two battalions—one known as "Wright's battalion," and the other as "Nethercutt's;" they had been in service as bridge guards or home guards, "local service;" they were combined as a regiment by an order. All the men in those local service companies not subject to conscription were to be discharged or transferred to other local service companies and assigned to duty as post guards, &c—that is, all not of the age, when subject to conscription. Those subject to conscription were taken out of these "local service" and "bridge guard" companies of "Nethercutt's" and "Wright's battalion," and put into the 66th North Carolina regiment. These "local service" and "bridge guard" companies had been organized before the conscription law had been enlarged as to the age of those liable to conscription.

Question. Were these local service and bridge guard companies, comprising "Nethercutt's" and "Wright's" battalions, in the confederate service?

Answer. My impression is they were; first in the State service and then transferred to the confederate service.

Question. State, if you please, what the terms of enlistment were in the original Nethercutt's battalion before going into the 66th.

Answer. I think they were "local service" companies for duty around Goldsborough and below; all State troops were liable under the laws of the State to go to any part of the State. I think they enlisted to go to any part of the State, though the private understanding was that they should be on duty below Goldsborough and vicinity. This private understanding would not appear on their muster-rolls.

Question. When they were in the confederate service, state whether they were still on duty as "Nethercutt's" battalion for local defence.

Answer. Yes. sir, they were, and under confederate pay; but how long they were under confederate pay I am unable to say.

Question. State whether "Nethercutt's battalion" were transferred to confederate authority subject to original terms of enlistment.

Answer. I dont recollect; when I was in command at Kinston, in fall of 1863, "Nethercutt's battalion" was there in its original condition. My impression is, they were transferred bodily to the 66th North Carolina at Kinston. All the men in "Nethercutt's battalion" were young men and liable to conscription, and were claimed, I think, by the war department at Richmond for general service.

Question. State whether the men of this battalion were given their choice of being sent to the conscription camp or joining the 66th North Carolina.

Answer. Yes, sir; all of both battalions were allowed to go to the conscription camp or remain in their organizations and enter the 66th North Carolina. "Wright's battalion" reorganized and elected new officers.

Question. State whether the confederate authorities claimed these men in "Nethercutt's battalion," before they were actually put into the 66th North Carolina, as being enlisted confederate soldiers or simply as North Carolinians liable to be conscripted under the confederate laws.

Answer. My impression is, they were in the confederate service in Nethercutt's battalion as "local service" troops. If these men were regularly in confederate service, they were so under the local service law of 1861. Nethercutt received authority, I believe, from the confederate authorities to organize these local companies into a battalion for "local service." Afterwards new conscript laws were made which would take in most of these men. To prevent disaffection, as these men were organized for local service in Nethercutt's battalion, the government would not break their engagements with them, and violate their terms of enlistment, and so gave the men their choice either to go to the conscript camp or into the 66th.

Question. State if one of the enlisted men in Nethercutt's battalion had refused to enter the 66th when so offered by the confederate authorities, but had left and gone home instead of to the conscript camp, whether he would have violated the terms of his enlistment in Nethercutt's battalion.

Answer. No, sir; not the terms of enlistment, but the conscript law and the orders under the conscript law, and under those orders been considered a deserter.

Question. State who gave the orders for the consolidation of Nethercutt's and other battalions into the 66th North Carolina, and who executed the consolidation?

Answer. I think the orders came from the war department of the Confederate States, and I executed them or caused them to be executed. They formed a part of my brigade. I think I recommended the consolidation previously.

Question. State whether there was any dissatisfaction expressed among the men of Nethercutt's battalion as to the consolidation into the 66th North Carolina regiment.

Answer. Yes, sir, there was, and the order given was not executed from that dissatisfaction at first, but subsequently they preferred to go into the 66th instead of being sent to the conscript camp. At one time Lieutenant Colonel Nethercutt and his men were opposed to it, and then there seemed to be a change of opinion, but what the cause of the change was I don't know.

Question. What were the expressed reasons of Colonel Nethercutt's dissatisfaction?

Answer. In the several interviews I had with him I don't recollect. I believe it was because I would not recommend him for the colonelcy, but of that I am not certain; this came to me through his friends. They did not want a regular officer over them, as Colonel A. D. Moore was, who became commandant of the 66th.

Question. State whether you recollect of any desertions from Nethercutt's battalion after the order for consolidation was given and before it was effected.

Answer. There were a few desertions, but the principal desertions took place after they were formed into the 66th, and when ordered to go from Kinston to Wilmington, North Carolina. I think they deserted then because they did not want to leave home.

Question. State whether all those of Nethercutt's battalion in the 66th voluntarily enlisted therein or were conscripted.

Answer. My impression is they went in voluntarily, rather than go to the conscript camp. My reason for this is that when the men were dissatisfied they generally came to me as their general, and none came with this complaint.

Question. State if any of Nethercutt's battalion were sent to the conscript camp instead of to the 66th.

Answer. I think none were sent there.

Question. State whether you know of the execution of any alleged deserters from the confederate service at Kinston in February, March, and April, 1864?

Answer. Only by hearsay. I never had any official order or other information connected with it. I was told at the time by some of the officers of the 66th who were of Nethercutt's battalion, that some of their men of Nethercutt's battalion had been court-martialled and shot at Kinston for desertion, but I never received any official record or saw the order approving proceedings of the court-martial. My brigade moved from Wilmington shortly after, and I never even heard that any information was sent to me or to the colonel of the regiment to which the men executed belonged.

Question. State whether the confederate authorities in enforcing the conscript law had authority to act upon local service organizations or simply on individuals.

Answer. Only on individuals in the local service organizations whose age and condition made them liable to the conscript law.

Question. State whether in forming the 66th an oath upon mustering in was taken by the men of Nethercutt's battalion.

Answer. No, sir; they simply signed the muster-in rolls of the 66th, which was the only formula ever used at that period of the war.

Question. State, please, who commanded at Kinston in February, March, and April, 1864.

Answer. I don't know.

The court adjourned until March 23, at 10 a. m, in order, if possible, to procure the attendance of Colonel B. Carter, supposed to have been a member of the military court before which the men executed were tried.

The court met pursuant to adjournment.

THURSDAY, *March* 23, 1866.

Eighteenth witness, Judge Battle, appeared and was sworn.

Question. State, please, your name, place of residence, and occupation.

Answer. My name is W. H. Battle, and I reside in Chapel Hill, North Carolina, and am one of the judges of the supreme court in the State of North Carolina, and professor at law in the university of the State at Chapel Hill.

Question. What was your occupation during the year 1864?

Answer. I was one of the judges of the supreme court.

Question. State whether in the latter part of 1863 and early part of 1864 you heard and decided any habeas corpus cases at chambers.

Answer. Yes; a number at different times.

Question. State whether you recollect any cases in which the petitioner claimed he was falsely claimed as a confederate soldier, when he claimed to belong to the "local service?"

Answer. Yes, sir; several from Lenoir county, and other localities, came before me claiming that they had volunteered for "local service," and had been taken off into the regular confederate service by General Hill. It was not pretended then that they had been conscripted under a conscription law. These petitioners, in every instance, some twenty or thirty, I discharged on habeas corpus on the grounds that they were subject to duty only for the local defence as bridge guards and other local organizations in which they had volunteered under the confederate act of congress as local confederate troops. This was in the summer and fall of 1863. I thought it was a very great outrage for General Hill to take them off. Afterwards other petitions were presented to me in about February, 1864, when returns were made that the petitioners were held under the confederate conscription act of January 5 and February 17, 1864, which was very sweeping in its character. The petitioners were therefore remanded into custody. The act of January 5 was in reference only to calling in those who had supplied substitutes.

Question. Do you recollect any cases which came before you in the latter part of 1863, or the early part of 1864, involving the legality of an order, purporting to emanate from the war department at Richmond, transferring certain local organizations known as "Nethercutt's battalion" or "partizan rangers" to the 66th North Carolina?

Answer. My impression is there were some few cases of that kind before me, but I do not think they raised any question as to the legality of that order; I do not think there were more than two or three before me. The ground of their objection to their discharge was set forth, I think, in the returns of their officers.

Question. State whether a record was kept of these decisions?

Answer. Yes, sir; but they were all transferred to the courts of record in order that the clerk might tax the costs under a section of our revised code.

Question. State whether you ever had any petitions from the 66th North Carolina for discharge on habeas corpus?

Answer. I received some, but do not recollect whether I ever received any before or after its consolidation as a regiment, or what disposition was made of them.

Question. State what you know of the execution of certain alleged deserters at Kinston, in February, March, or April, in the year 1864.

Answer. I know nothing whatever, personal or official, except by mere rumor, residing, as I did at the time, far removed from the theatre of active military operations, in eastern North Carolina.

Question. State whether you know as to who commanded in those months in eastern North Carolina.

Answer. I do not know.

The nineteenth witness, John C. Gorman, appeared and was sworn.

Question. State your name, residence, and occupation.

Answer. My name is John C. Gorman; I am a printer by occupation, and reside in Raleigh, North Carolina.

Question. What was your occupation in the early part of 1864.

Answer. I was captain 2d North Carolina infantry, on duty in Virginia.

Question. State what you know of the executions of alleged deserters at Kinston in February, March and April, 1864.

Answer. I know nothing; I was at home in Raleigh, then on sick leave, having been wounded, and went down one day to Kinston for provisions for my family, but I know nothing of these occurrences.

Colonel Carter sworn as twentieth witness:

Question. State your name, age, and place of residence.

Answer. David Miller Carter; thirty-six years of age, and reside in the town of Washington, Beaufort county, North Carolina, and am a lawyer.

Question. What was your occupation in the months of February, March and April, 1864, and where were you stationed?

Answer. I was a colonel of cavalry, assigned to duty as presiding judge of a military court, third corps, army of northern Virginia, Confederate States service. I was stationed on the southern bank of the Rapidan river, in Virginia.

Question. State whether you were, during that period, in the State of North Carolina at any time.

Answer. No, sir; I was not. I went to Virginia in June, 1861, with the 4th North Carolina regiment, and never returned again until May, 1864, on leave of absence, and in August I resigned my commission, to enter the State legislature to which I have been re-elected.

Question. State whether you know anything connected with the capture and execution of certain alleged deserters from the rebel army at Kinston?

Answer. I have no knowledge, either personal or official. I was in Virginia at the time, and derived the slight information I did have from the newspapers, in which were published the correspondence between Major General John Peck, commanding the United States forces in North Carolina, and Major General G. E. Pickett, commanding the confederate forces in eastern North Carolina. I have had the reputation of having been engaged in these transactions, which has caused me great inconvenience and undeserved obloquy, which is totally without foundation.

Several other witnesses were examined, whose testimony, being entirely irrelevant, is herein omitted.

We hereby certify that the foregoing testimony is correct as taken by this board.

Dated Raleigh, North Carolina, March 29, 1866.

       ASA BIRD GARDNER,
    First Lieut. and Adj't 7th Reg't V. R. C.
      and President Board of Inquiry.
    GEORGE H. PENNIMAN,
  First Lieut. 28th Mich. Inft'y Vol. and Recorder.
      WM. R. WILCOX,
   Second Lieut. Co. K, 28th Mich. Inft'y Vols.

RALEIGH, N. C., *March* 30, 1866.

The board having met and deliberated as to the possibility of obtaining further evidence, decided to adjourn *sine die*, and accordingly so adjourned.

ASA BIRD GARDNER,
*First Lieut. and Adj't 7th Reg't V. R. C. and
President Board of Inquiry.*
GEO. H. PENNIMAN,
First Lieut. 28th Mich. Vol. Inf'y and Recorder.
Brevet Maj. Gen. S. H. RUGER,
Commanding Dep't of North Carolina, Raleigh, N. C.

List of witnesses.

	Page.
First witness, John B. Neathery, A. A. G.	61
Second witness, Ed. B. Freeman, clerk supreme court	63
Third witness, Geo. Snow, A. D. C.	64
Fourth witness, S. McD. Tate, Lieut. Col. 6th N. C	67
Fifth witness, —— Engelhardt, clerk State senate	70
Sixth witness, Oscar Eastmond, Col. 1st Loyal N. C. Vols	70
Seventh witness, Caleb Gaylord	70
Eighth witness, John Hughes, Brig. Q. M	70
Ninth witness, Jno. N. Whitford, Col. 67th N. C	71
Tenth witness, Zebulon B. Vance, ex-governor	72
Eleventh witness, Jno. G. Justice, A. D. C.	73
Twelfth witness, Wm. G. Lewis, brigadier general	75
Thirteenth witness, Jno. C. Washington, planter	76
Fourteenth witness, Geo. W. Quinn, mil. courier	77
Fifteenth witness, Blunt King, hangman	79
Sixteenth witness, Drury Lacy, Adj't 43d N. C	81
Seventeenth witness, James G. Martin, brigadier general	83
Eighteenth witness, Wm. H. Battle, judge supreme court	86
Nineteenth witness, John C. Gorman, captain 2d N. C.	87
Twentieth witness, D. M. Carter, Col. Cav	87

Official:
W. A. NICHOLS,
Assistant Adjutant General.

No. 12.

HEADQUARTERS DEPARTMENT OF NORTH CAROLINA,
Raleigh, North Carolina, April 17, 1866.

GENERAL: I have the honor to state that, in the investigation of the facts relating to certain alleged murders said to have taken place at Kinston, North Carolina, of soldiers of the United States, by execution at the hands of the rebels, which I was directed by indorsement of the Secretary of War, of date December 15, 1865, to investigate, it is necessary to a full knowledge of the matter that the court-martial proceedings had by the rebels in the case be examined. I would therefore request, if the same be among the rebel archives, that I be furnished a copy of the record in the cases of Joseph L. Haskett, David Jones, Mitchell Busick, William Irvine, Amos Aymett, Lewis Bryan, John J. Brock, William Haddock, Jesse J. Summerlin, Andrew J. Britton, Lewis Freeman.

MURDER OF UNION SOLDIERS IN NORTH CAROLINA. 89

Calvin J. Hoffman, Stephen J. Jones, Joseph Brock, Lewis Taylor, Chas, Cutherville, William H. Dougherty, and Elijah Kellum, tried at Kinston, North Carolina, in the spring of 1864, and executed as deserters from the rebel army.

The rebel General Pickett commanded the department of east North Carolina, and probably ordered the execution.

Very respectfully, your obedient servant,
THOMAS H. KUGER,
Bvt. Maj. Gen. Vols., Commanding.

Bvt. Maj. Gen. E. D. TOWNSEND,
Ass't Adj't Gen. U. S. A., Washington, D. C.

Respectfully referred to Dr. Francis Leiber, chief of the Bureau of Records and Archives, who will please inform this office if the proceedings called for within are among the files of rebel archives.

W. A. NICHOLS,
Assistant Adjutant General.

ADJUTANT GENERAL'S OFFICE, *April* 21, 1866.

Respectfully returned. The proceedings referred to are not among the records of this office. Enclosed are the only papers that can be found relating to the execution.

G. NORMAN LIEBER,
Bvt. Lt. Col. in absence of chief A. S.

ARCHIVE OFFICE, *Washington, April* 25, 1866.

Official:

W. A. NICHOLS,
Assistant Adjutant General.

Ex. Doc. 98——7

www.ingramcontent.com/pod-product-compliance
Lightning Source LLC
Chambersburg PA
CBHW020259090426
42735CB00009B/1148